LEXICON OF

BALCONIES AND PATIO PLANTS

A guide to successful and creative planting

WOTA WEHMEYER &

HERMANN HACKSTEIN

REBO PRODUCTIONS

Contents

Foreword

ENJOY A LOVELIER LIVING ENVIRONMENT WITH BALCONY AND PATIO PLANTS

You will scarcely ever find a garden, a patio, or a balcony without them—balcony and patio plants. They bring a little nature into our built-up environment, create colorful feasts for the eyes, and, with their incredible range of species and varieties, offer an endless source of fascination. So it is hardly surprising that they are, quite simply, among our most popular plants.

In saying that, "patio plants" are by no means a particular species or variety in the strictly botanical sense. Rather, this is a generic term for plants that can be grown equally well in boxes or tubs as in beds.

The term "patio plant" mainly characterizes the non-hardy types that have to be over-wintered in sheltered conditions in colder regions—it is thus an advantage for them to be easily transportable in containers. The term is also commonly used, however, for any larger plants such as shrubs and trees that are too big for flowerpots, hanging baskets, or flower troughs.

Central to this whole category are those that are suitable for hanging baskets and troughs, their magnificent blooms providing an indulgent treat for the eyes.

No matter what the precise definition of balcony and patio plants, however, ultimately just about any kind is suitable for growing and keeping in a container, provided it is big enough.

In a small handbook, we have had to be selective, putting emphasis on some plants rather than others. In this respect, the authors have been guided less by botanical considerations than by the needs of most "mini-gardeners," irrespective of whether they "only" want to plant a small balcony, brighten up a sill with a window box, or make a patio more interesting with tubs.

The priority for us is not just a fascination with plants themselves, or their landscaping possibilities, but practical questions and needs. We focus our attention more on a plant that provides visual cover with low maintenance, for example, than on a rare exotic that would fill a professional gardener with excitement.

On this basis, we hope that you enjoy this book and have plenty of successful "green" experiences!

Little plant paradises

Versatile companions

LIVING WITH BALCONY AND PATIO PLANTS

There are as many reasons for deciding on portable planters as there are suitable plants for pots, baskets, boxes, and tubs.

Lovers of flowers and foliage, for example, delight in the fact that balcony and patio planting enables even exotic specimens to flourish in colder regions. Cooks value the constant availability of fresh herbs. Architects use planters as design features; garden lovers draw attention with them; and people in need of relaxation can create a small oasis of nature with them. The list is endless.

There can be no doubt that one of the greatest advantages of balcony and patio plants is their ability to introduce a little bit of nature into our urban landscape within a very small area. Whether it is flower boxes on windowsills, hanging baskets beside balcony doors, or planters on the patio,

balcony and patio plants bring greenery closer to buildings than is usually possible with gardens. Moreover, they even flourish in a setting where nature does not normally have much space to develop.

Yet the popularity of balcony and patio plants is hard to imagine without their ornamental qualities. From the first glimpse of spring until late fall, plants laden with blooms spoil us with their magnificent splashes of color. Tulips, narcissi, geraniums, petunias, dahlias and asters—all year round they enrich our lives and provide us with an attractive visual focus. Unlike the members of the same species firmly set in flowerbeds and front gardens, with balcony and patio plants it is possible to create completely new plant scenarios from one year to the next. This is not just by constant new planting and changing color schemes: by reorganizing specific containers or altering arrangements of groups of planters, you can achieve quite different displays from season to season.

Other creative advantages are that balcony and patio plants fit into any garden design and can even enhance and distinguish it. You only have to think of gardens laid out in a Mediterranean style. They are unimaginable without oleander, citrus plants, and bougainvillea—all of them non-perennials that cannot over-winter outside at colder latitudes.

Even the image of the romantic cottage garden is directly associated with container plants, whether they are herbs such as parsley and chives or shrubs and annuals like touch-me-nots and dahlias.

The design strengths of balcony and patio plants can be put to good use in many different ways. When sympathetically positioned on terraces, for example, they can create a seamless transition between house and garden.

Larger or more eye-catching plants do not just attract our attention, but can also direct it—for example, to access routes and entrances. So a favorite configuration of balcony and patio plants is to frame doors with two identical plants. This type of layout even has special significance in feng shui, the harmonizing, Oriental design doctrine that sees them as "guards."

In terms of access routes, balcony and patio plants can also serve as attractive boundary markers to show where paths divide, for instance. Scattering small tubs on steps is also a very decorative touch.

Balcony and patio plants are also useful for concealing less attractive spots such as manhole covers or grates over cellar chutes. Nearer the house, they are ideal for camouflaging drainpipes or unappealing niches.

Containers and hanging baskets are also a good way of breaking up large areas of wall space, especially if the plants grow against espaliers or trellises. Positioned against balcony and terrace walls and planted in wide containers, they provide windbreaks and visual cover—it is even quite easy to create "green walls" using this technique. Performing the same function, they can also be placed on garden terraces or in front of sunrooms and summerhouses.

The list of the practical sides of patio plants could go on indefinitely. Ambitious gardeners like to bury tubs in the ground in order to control, for example, the spread of grasses like bamboo. No matter what their function, however, the plants themselves are always the most important factor. They are the stars of the show, providing the real thrills with the rich diversity of their movements and features.

Creating with skill

SETTING THE RIGHT SCENE

The effectiveness of balcony and patio plants is determined by many factors. Particularly important are, on the one hand, the height of the vegetation and the planters used and, on the other, the surrounding surfaces and background.

As a basic principle, we consider layouts with balcony and patio plants successful if they captivate. A small plant standing alone in a wide-open space such as a large patio looks lonely and lost. The eye overlooks it in the literal sense of the word. By contrast, if you arrange several small plants compactly in a larger container to make a colorful ensemble, they move naturally into the line of vision. You only have to think of the magnificent splendor of geraniums in window boxes that everyone loves.

Whether you combine several plants of the same species or completely different

ones is really a matter of personal taste. If you choose different plants, it is of course vital that they like the same levels of sun or shade and prefer similar types of soil conditions.

Neither is it a question of only combining a few small plants, for many larger plants that grow to a good height—especially those with stems—are excellent for planting among smaller ones that can act as groundcover.

The dimensions needed for an arrangement to catch the eye are determined by the size of the surrounding space. On a balcony measuring only a few square feet, even small plant groupings can create a pleasing effect that would be lost in larger areas.

Basically, there are two different approaches to designing layouts with balcony and patio plants—one aims at producing the most spectacular appearance for the plants and their arrangement, while the other seeks to integrate them in the most natural way with their environment.

The kind of approach to choose depends above all on the style of the garden. The more naturally this is laid out, the less obtrusively the plants should be integrated. The planter is a vital factor in this process, as it allows you to create deliberately contrasting effects.

INSEPARABLE COUPLES

Plants on the one hand and the container on the other—together they form an indivisible, artistic whole. Small highlights in the garden can be created through the skillful combination of both. Conversely, however, the wrong plant in the wrong pot or tub can look completely out of place. Decisive factors are not only the size and shape, but also the color and material of the containers.

The most important factor is, of course, that the container offers the plant or plants enough room to grow. Just how big the tub or box has to be in order to do this will vary from plant to plant. Deep-rooted plants like roses need very tall pots, while other plants that may actually be bigger are far less demanding in terms of container depth.

Stability also has an important part to play. The rule of thumb is that, the higher the plant grows, the wider and heavier its container needs to be. Trees and shrubs, but also

substantial plant arrangements, are particularly demanding in this respect.

Personal taste should not be the sole factor determining the choice of container. A successful design blends harmoniously with its surroundings, whether with the architecture, the layout of the garden or, best of all, with both. So containers with straight, clean lines fit well into a setting based on modern designs. Rounded containers, on the other hand, emphasize a romantic ambiance, while terracotta pots go hand in hand with a Mediterranean garden. If pot or tubs are placed on pedestals, the same of course applies.

Play of colors is also important for the effect, and here

the shades of both plants and containers have to harmonize. So combinations of pink, red, and violet can often be difficult, while distinct colors like blue, red, and yellow go well together—and with white, as well.

To be on the safe side, it is best to choose containers in earth colors like beige or terracotta or neutral tones like white. In this case, however, the effect tends to be unremarkable. By contrast, using a spectacular color for its container can showcase a plant that would otherwise perhaps be lost in the overall design.

Another factor in choosing plant containers relates to what the pot, box, basket, or tub is actually made of. Here, too, the focus should remain on the overall look—contemporary materials like lacquered tin, stainless steel, or concrete always look better in a modern context than in historical or Mediterranean-style surroundings. For the latter, opt for containers in natural materials such as earthenware or wood.

While the choice of plant containers was limited to a few standard products until a few years ago, the selection nowadays is immense. Above all, a great deal has been done in terms of shape and substance. From unusually woven branches or combinations of materials in glass and plastic, to wall planters in the style of antique statues or custom-designed containers, the range on offer is virtually endless.

But even the huge selection of ready-made items pales in comparison with the creativity that many gardeners use to produce a really individual effect for their balcony and patio plants. Old handbags and shoes, cars and bikes—it seems you can use anything that holds earth or can accommodate a planter.

The right plants

A GREAT SELECTION, BUT NOT MUCH SPACE

On balconies and patios the available space for plants in flower boxes is usually very limited, so the choice between the many patio plants on offer is a difficult one.

This makes it all the more important to have a clear idea beforehand of the realistic plant options and to pay close attention to the space needs and growth height of the plants when buying them in a specialist garden center.

> ### TOP TEN
> ### HANGING BASKETS AND
> ### BALCONY BOXES
>
> - Begonia hybrids (begonias)
> - Bidens (Beggarticks)
> - Diascia hybrids (figwort)
> - Fuchsias
> - Impatiens
> - Lobelia
> - Pelargoniums (geraniums)
> - Petunia hybrids (petunias)
> - Scaevola (naupaka)
> - Verbena hybrids (vervain)

HANGING BASKETS AND FLOWER BOXES

They are considered some of the great classics among patio plants—flowers for hanging baskets and balcony boxes. The best plants for these are above all the ones that catch the eye with their overhanging mass of blooms. When planting in spring, it is essential to give the young plants enough room to develop and not to position them too close to each other in the container; this way, they will grow rapidly and in great profusion. It is also important to measure the exact amount when watering—just as too much water causes damage, so does too little. In addition, the plants need to be given fertilizer regularly, with faded flowers being removed on a regular basis.

CLIMBERS AND CREEPERS

Large plant containers and sturdy supports are the key to success when climbers and creepers are being used to add greenery to walls or for camouflage. Young shoots must be trained in the direction you want at an early stage. Better results will be obtained by regular pruning, especially of shoots that are growing the wrong way. When tying them back, be careful not to fasten the knots of the twine and cord too tightly, or you might damage the plants.

TOP TEN CLIMBERS AND CREEPERS

- Actinidia chinensis
- Aristolochia durior
- Bougainvillea
- Campsis radicans
- Clematis
- Jasmine
- Passiflora
- Plumbago
- Thunbergia alata
- Vitis vinifera

MEDITERRANEAN GARDENS

They create a southern flair and a touch of holiday mood on balconies and patios—the non-perennial plants known as "exotics." Before buying them, you should be quite sure of what is needed to over-winter the plants.

During the cold season, many of them need a dry, moderately warm, and bright position. What should also be considered is that most of these non-perennials reach an impressive height of over 6ft (2 m) with the correct care. This also means that they need increasingly large pots through time, and therefore become far heavier. This can often lead, not only to problems with the plants themselves, but also with moving them around.

TOP TEN MEDITERRANEAN FLAIR

- Aloe
- Brugmansia
- Camellia japonica
- Citrus
- Cymbidium
- Erythrina crista-galli
- Ficus carica
- Lavandula
- Nerium oleander
- Strelitzia reginae

SMALL KITCHEN GARDENS

Herbs, fruit, and vegetables—balcony and patio plants can be more than just decoration. All the same, they enrich not only your cuisine, but also the visual image of the plants, with their decorative leaf shapes, pretty blossoms, and plump fruits.

And there is always space for herbs, even on the tiniest balcony. Many herbs—such as basil, parsley, and chives—are very sensitive and should be given a sheltered spot, especially away from rain. Not only people like certain herbs: snails in particular love parsley and basil.

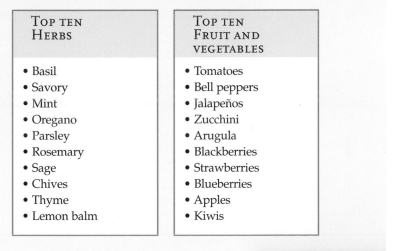

TOP TEN HERBS	TOP TEN FRUIT AND VEGETABLES
• Basil	• Tomatoes
• Savory	• Bell peppers
• Mint	• Jalapeños
• Oregano	• Zucchini
• Parsley	• Arugula
• Rosemary	• Blackberries
• Sage	• Strawberries
• Chives	• Blueberries
• Thyme	• Apples
• Lemon balm	• Kiwis

These plants should be hung up in patio areas, or their containers at least raised off the ground, to make them less accessible.

As for fruit, stores now stock a wide selection of container varieties that will yield an abundant, delicious harvest. With berries, thorn-free specimens are recommended, especially where space is tight. With skillful work, grape vines, kiwis, and blackberries can provide a screen as well as a windbreak. For kitchen gardens, the bigger the pot, the bigger the chance of enjoying a good harvest.

Potting plants

HOW TO POT PLANTS PROFESSIONALLY

For plants to flourish, it is essential to plant them professionally in pots, tubs, and boxes. They can only survive if they have enough space, a regular supply of plant food, and protection from excess ground water.

To get maximum enjoyment from beautiful balcony and patio plants, the planting stage plays a very important role. Many plants fail to thrive, or do not reach their full potential, if they are planted or repotted too early or too late. Hot days with strong sunshine are also unfavorable conditions for planting.

In practice, it is best to be guided by what is available in market gardens or garden centers. Sellers usually only offer those plants that can be set at the time of purchase. So, for example, plants that should be potted in summer are only available in the stores during the summer months. If you are unsure, try and consult an expert member of staff for advice when buying.

A newly acquired plant needs to be put into a suitable potting mix—as the soil is called—and, of course, a nice container that is the right size for the plant.

THE CORRECT SOIL

Plants need different things from the ground in which they are meant to flourish. Some of them, for instance, need a more acid base; others prefer sandy soil; yet others require a chalky environment for ideal growth.

As a rule, normal topsoil does not fulfill these requirements. So trade stores offer a wide selection of different types of soil for plants, some of which are quite specific to certain plants, such as roses or geraniums. For most plants, however, simple potting compost will serve perfectly well. This type of standard potting mix is not expensive and is usually free from weed seeds; it is also alkaline-neutral, with a pH value of about 7. Moreover, if it becomes obvious at a later stage that the standard mix is not meeting the needs of the plants—e.g., they are growing too slowly—you can always rectify this by, for example, adding a selected fertilizer.

The plant container

It is important that the size of the container matches the needs of the plant and is proportionate to its size. If it is too small, there will not be enough potting mix to provide the plant with all the nutrients it needs. If it is not deep enough, there is the danger of the plant becoming waterlogged— water gathers at the bottom of the planter, threatening the roots. A large container also provides stability for plants that grow to a good height and then become heavier. A tub or box can in fact only be far too big from an aesthetic point of view. A rule of thumb is: the pot should be at least 20 percent bigger than the root ball—in the case of a ball measuring 4 ins (10 cm) deep and wide, the pot should be at least 5 x 5 ins (12 x 12 cm).

Used clay pots should be scrubbed free of any residue with a wire brush before any new planting, to get rid of any pests. Unglazed, new clay pots should be soaked in water before use, so that they do not absorb excess moisture from the earth at a later stage.

TOOLS

For both potting and re-potting you will need a trowel for relocating young plants. A dustpan and brush is also useful for clearing up excess soil after planting.

A pair of strong scissors can come in handy for cutting up plastic pots. If you want to break up old pots for essential drainage, keep a small hammer close to hand. It is best to work with gardening gloves, especially in the case of thorny plants. A watering can is recommended for watering your plants.

STEP-BY-STEP GUIDE TO POTTING

1. DRAINAGE

First of all, some form of drainage system has to be placed in the pot, tub, or box to allow excess water to flow off properly at a later stage and prevent the plant becoming waterlogged. The system consists of a layer of solid material that covers the bottom of the container without blocking the drainage hole. Material used for larger pots can be broken pieces of earthenware and, for smaller ones, pebbles or pieces of bark.

2. FILLING WITH SOIL

On top of the drainage system, add soil to the level at which the root ball of the plant will sit just under the rim of the pot. The soil bought in bags is usually packed tightly, so it is a good idea to break up large chunks by hand.

3. FERTILIZER

The soil can now be enriched: for example, with an all-purpose fertilizer. This should be mixed through the potting soil by hand.

4. REMOVE THE PLANT

The next step is to loosen the root ball of the plant by gently pressing, turning, or tapping it out of its plastic housing. If this does not work, or the roots have already grown through the drainage holes, the plastic should be cut away with scissors. Take care not to damage the roots in the process! Then loosen the root ball with your hand, so that the roots are no longer tightly packed and can grow better in the new potting mix.

5. Potting your plant

Now place the plant carefully into the tub, adjusting it to the correct position. With larger plants, it is best to leave a gap between the plant and the sides of the container. Fill up this space with some loose potting mix, pack it down to set the plant firmly in place, and add some more soil if required.

6. Watering

Next, water the soil carefully near to the roots so that the plant can take root and compact itself into the potting mix. A watering can is very useful for measuring the right amount of water.

7. Topping up with soil

Finally, top up with soil, pressing it down firmly. Do not fill the pot right to the top edge, or the soil will spill over when you water the plant.

This also leaves enough space for a separate layer to cover the soil. This can consist of bark mulch, decorative pebbles, or coconut chips. A layer like this is a good idea for larger tubs with lots of visible soil surface, and not just for aesthetic reasons. It also helps to retain moisture and protect sensitive plant roots—such as those of the clematis—from too much sunlight. In the first few days after potting, keep a close eye on the plant and, in particular, ensure that it is sufficiently watered.

Proper care

THE ART OF WATERING

For your balcony and patio plants to flourish, you have to nourish and tend them correctly. Above all, this means adding the right amount of water and fertilizer and keeping the soil free from weeds. In addition, many plants need to be supported or pruned and regularly repotted. Spotting pests and diseases early and taking swift remedial action is important.

Correct watering is not always easy, however, especially with balcony and patio plants: water evaporates more rapidly than in a bed, but you cannot water too much or the plants will become waterlogged. Rain is not necessarily a friend to container plants, as thick foliage often prevents the water reaching the root balls. On the other hand, real flooding can develop if it rains too persistently.

A general rule: the bigger the plant and the more potting mix it has, the simpler the watering regime. Small plant

containers—especially hanging baskets and flower boxes—
normally only have a small amount of soil, so it is necessary
to provide moisture with particular care.

A basic principle: in hot, sunny weather, tubs, baskets,
and wall containers should be watered twice a day. You can
test whether the plant needs water by sticking your finger
into the soil—if it is dry down to 1 in (3 cm), you must water
it immediately!

On hot, summer days it is also extremely important to
water only the soil and not the plant itself. Drops of water
act like a magnifying glass, intensifying the rays of the sun
and burning the leaves of the plant as a result.

ADDING FERTILIZER CORRECTLY

For balcony and patio plants to do well and look their best, they should regularly be given fertilizer. Even if you added a base fertilizer when originally potting plants that are now mature—e.g., over a year old—you must top up with fertilizer occasionally, to ensure the plant receives enough nutrients.

There are various types of fertilizer. First of all, there is the distinction between organic and inorganic media. The most common organic fertilizer used in gardens is compost. It not only provides nutrients, but also loosens up the subsoil and improves its texture.

Inorganic fertilizers are produced synthetically and provide the plant with minerals such as phosphates, nitrogen, and potassium. As well as standard fertilizers, there are also special mixes—for roses, azaleas, and tomatoes, for example. These take account of the specific needs of certain

plants. All types of fertilizer are available in different forms, such as granules, sticks, tablets, or fluid concentrate. The so-called "slow release" fertilizers gradually release the nutrients into the soil; the good quality ones can provide the plants with nutrients for a whole summer. Take care not to over fertilize, however.

LASTING CARE

With most plants, small-scale interventions are constantly needed in terms of care, especially during the flowering season. So dried-out blooms and damaged or dead shoots should be removed to give the plant strength and space for new flowers and growth, as well as to maintain its beautiful appearance.

The same applies to weeds: for one thing, unwanted and uncultivated plants (as they are sometimes described) are not a very pretty sight. For another, they rob the soil of nutrients and can even damage or choke balcony and patio plants. For this reason, unwanted "strangers" should be removed regularly from plant containers.

SUPPORTING AND MAINTAINING YOUR PLANTS

Many tall-growing plants need some form of support for their development—above all, of course, climbing plants. But even with roses or tomatoes, supports are advisable. They prevent, for instance, shoots from breaking under the excess weight of fruit or flowers.

There is a huge selection of supports catering to the needs of different types of plants. Climbers require vertical supports like poles, ropes, or wires. Creepers prefer trellises made of covered wire, rope, or wood, while rambling plants like roses prefer a frame with as many horizontal parts as possible. For fruit species, it is best to use espaliers.

SELECTIVE PRUNING

Regular pruning of shoots promotes the proliferation of a plant. Thus two new shoots usually develop, if you make the cut above a bud. This kind of cutting back helps to support the formation of new flowers, fruit yield, or denser growth.

When, and how exactly, to do the pruning varies considerably from plant to plant. Some plants bloom a second time if you cut them back after the first flowering, while many patio plants are not pruned until late fall before over-wintering.

As well as cutting back, structural pruning is recommended for some plants to give a particular visual effect. In doing this, new shoots can be shortened and tied firmly to encourage future growth in the direction you want. This is especially popular with box trees and conifers, which people like to shape into spheres and pyramids. Another option is the crowned tree: first, trim back all the side shoots till the plant reaches the desired height, using a support pole. Then cut the top off and nip off the side shoots at regular intervals to encourage multiple branching.

OVER-WINTERING

With the exception of a few perennials, most balcony and patio plants do not survive the winter without some precautionary measures. Frost poses the greatest threat to them: the containers cool down quickly and the water in them freezes, with earthenware pots being particularly likely to break in these conditions.

Most non-hardy plants should be moved to a bright, cool position at the beginning of the cold season, preferably unheated, but with a temperature no lower than 32 °F (0° C). Suitable places are stairwells and, of course, winter gardens. In addition, there are a few plants that should be cut back completely and then over-wintered in the dark: for example, in a cellar or garage.

Large plants that have to over-winter out of doors should firstly be put in the most sheltered position possible—beside walls, in alcoves, or behind screens or other windbreaks. The best thing is to pack up the tub or box with plastic bubble wrap. To do this, wrap the packaging material several times around the container and secure it at the top with wire. Alternatively, you can protect your container plants against the cold with straw or rushes. In either case,

the planters should not be in direct contact with the ground, but placed on polystyrene sheets.

For over-wintering, it is extremely important to pay attention to the moisture level of the soil. As a rule, the plants should be watered every four to six weeks. Otherwise, they will dry out. With plants that need to be over-wintered in sunlight, such as palms, frequent watering is usually required.

It is crucial to protect the plants from the first frost and not put them back in the open too early. No matter how mild, or even warm, some days in March can be, there is always the danger of cold spells until at least the middle of May.

REPOTTING

Plants do not just grow visibly upward and outward: their roots spread and propagate as well. This means that balcony and patio plants normally need a larger receptacle after two to three years. Otherwise, there is an increased risk of water logging, as the roots grow down into the drainage area. In addition, and in particular, tall, heavy plants can become unstable. The nutrients in the soil also

become depleted over time, so a fresh base fertilizer should be added to the new pot. The steps for repotting are just the same as those for initial planting (see page 36).

To remove a plant from its pot, hold it at the bottom if possible and tap carefully around the edge of the pot with a piece of wood. If you cannot loosen the root ball this way, run a knife vertically around the top between the root system and the edge of the pot. If the roots have already grown through the hole in the bottom of the container, you can cut these away without damaging the plant.

Then place the root ball into its new, larger container.

A–Z of plants

Selecting the plants

THE RIGHT PLANT

Apart from a small number of very large trees—for example, the oak or sequoia—just about any plant can be kept in a pot or tub, provided the chosen container is big enough. As a result, you will find an incredibly broad spectrum of plants on balconies and patios across the world.

In saying this, there is still a whole range of plants particularly suited to containers in all their different forms. In over 120 plant portraits in the following pages, we will give you an introduction to the most important ones.

This selection cannot make any claim to comprehensive ness, but reflects instead the personal preferences of the authors. Some portraits give a more extensive outline of certain subspecies that are particularly appropriate for balconies and patios, and/or enjoy widespread popularity.

THE INFORMATION BOXES

To make it easier to choose your own plant paradise, a small information box has been included in each plant portrait. The first line indicates the preferred position, the symbol(s) showing whether the plant prefers full sun, partial shade, or total shade.

The second line gives the height of the fully-grown plant, which can of course vary considerably depending on the species. In several portraits, the information relates to the most common varieties of the plant, while indications as to which species potentially grow taller or shorter can be found in the text.

Finally, the flowering period, where applicable, is indicated in months (Roman numerals beside a flower symbol).

Acer palmatum

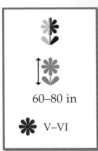

60–80 in

V–VI

Japanese Maple

Particularly toward the end of the summer, when the magnificent blooms on balconies and patios are slowly fading, you will get plenty of enjoyment from the wonderful fall colors of the Japanese Maple. The characteristic leaf shape is

undoubtedly responsible for the botanical name Acer, which comes from Latin and means "sharp" or "pointed."

The Japanese Maple, with its habitually broad, arching growth, produces purple-red flowers from May through June followed by red fruit in late summer. The fresh, green, summer color of the leaves—with varying depths of lobe depending on the variety—transforms in the fall into highly ornamental, vibrant shades of yellow, orange, and red.

If you plant this attractive, deciduous tree in a box or tub, be sure to choose low-growing varieties. The delicate "dissectum" cultivars are particularly suitable in this respect, growing to approximately 60–80 in (150–200 cm). A few examples are "dissectum atropurpureum" (elegant, burgundy leaves with tapering lobes); "dissectum garnet" (deep-red leaves); and "dissectum nigrum" (deep mahogany leaves).

Acer palmatum, which should be given a spot in partial shade sheltered from the wind, prefers fresh, humus-rich soil.

Agapanthus

LILY OF THE NILE

The most distinctive feature of this well-loved tub plant, originally native to South Africa, is its umbellate florescence on erect, leafless stems. These flowers make the Agapanthus, which is also commonly known as the African Lily and the Flower of Love, a real eye-catcher on a balcony or patio.

Stems around 40 in (100 cm) tall rise out of a thick clump of slender, strap-shaped leaves that project perkily over the edge of the container. From July through September, ornamental umbels appear on these tall stems in a mass of small, funnel-shaped flowers. Most are blue, but they also can be white. Depending on the species and cultivar, the plant can reach heights of 28–60 in (70–150 cm).

Agapanthus should stand in a sheltered spot, in full sun. This plant does best in rich, well-drained soil and should be watered and fertilized liberally. Take care that it does not become water-logged, however, to avoid rot in the fleshy roots. It is best to choose a sizeable, very sturdy container, as the powerful roots of this plant could otherwise burst it.

Some examples of well-known species are Agapanthus praecox, Agapanthus africanus, and Agapanthus companulatus.

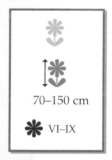

70–150 cm

✳ VI–IX

Agave americana

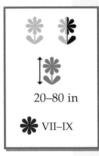

20–80 in

VII–IX

AGAVE

Agaves are extremely versatile plants that combine very well with many others, especially spectacular, flowering container plants. Its impressive leaves can serve either as a background effect or special focal point.

The evergreen Agave forms striking, bluish-green rosettes of broad, lanceolate leaves with spiny margins. You have to be lucky and very patient to experience the flowering of an Agave, as it takes about 10–15 years in its natural habitat, even under ideal conditions, for the plant to finally produce flowers. These are yellow, and appear on very long stems. After flowering, the mother plant then dies off. Agave americana can reach an overall height of 20–80 in (50–200 cm).

Originally native to dry regions of Mexico and the Mediterranean, Agave is a member of the Succulent family. This means it can store water in its leaves, so it should only be watered sparingly. This plant loves heat, preferring a sunny position if possible. Failing this, choose a spot in partial shade and sheltered from rain. Care is advised when handling agaves, as it is easy to be "bitten" by the sharp spines on its leaves.

Allium schoenoprasum

ca. 12 in

❋ V–VII

CHIVE

Related to the onion, but with a far subtler taste, Chive is universally known and loved as a culinary herb. Freshly picked, it is a delicious addition to eggs, sauces, soups, salads, curd cheese, and potato or fish dishes. Chive is said to stimulate the appetite and aid digestion. In addition, the green culms are highly ornamental and often used as a garnish.

Mature plants can reach a height of about 12 in (30 cm). The tubular leaves are of varying thickness, depending on the species. From May through August, ornamental flower heads in shades from deep violet to dark pink appear on the

grassy clumps, providing lovely accents in flower boxes. Some of the prettiest varieties include the white-flowering "Corsican White" and the red-flowering "Forescate."

You have to decide, however, whether your Chive is to be used as decoration or as an herb; as the florescence saps strength from the plant, it should, if appropriate, be removed in good time.

On balconies and patios, Chive prefers a moderately warm position in full sun to partial shade. It thrives best in loamy, humus-rich garden soil.

When picking, cut the little tubes a couple of inches above the ground and then wait until they grow back again. Chive should not be chopped, but cut—if possible with a sharp knife—and sprinkled over food just before serving. It can also be used as a dried herb, but it loses some of its aroma this way.

There is now also the so-called Chinese Chive (Allium tuberosum), a cross between chives and garlic. The care is the same, with the plant attaining a height of 16–20 in (40–50 cm).

Aloe

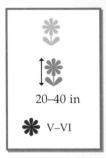

20–40 in

❋ V–VI

ALOE

The Aloe genus is made up of a large number of different types of evergreen shrubs, most of which are native to Africa, Madagascar, and Arabia. A typical feature of Aloes is the succulent leaves in which they store water, enabling them to survive lengthy dry spells. Thus they adapted ideally to the living conditions in their original environment.

Even in more temperate climes, Aloes prefer a warm, bright, dry position in the sun. The plant does not need a great deal of water; its soil just needs to be kept slightly damp. During the winter season, the plants need even less moisture. Care must therefore be taken when watering, as soaking the roots can easily lead to rot.

As tub plants, Aloes are well suited to creating exotic, desert-like landscapes on balconies and patios. It is worth mentioning two of the many species:

ALOE VERA: The best-known species of Aloe must be Aloe vera—the Real Aloe. It is appreciated, not only for its substantial ornamental value, but also for the sap of its leaves, to which medicinal, relaxing, and cosmetic properties are attributed. It grows to a height of about 20–24 in (50–60 cm) and consists of a stem-less rosette of lanceolate, fleshy, grayish-green leaves. The tubular yellow flowers grow in racemes in terminal clusters.

ALOE STRIATA: Aloe striata is an almost stemless succulent with a dense rosette of lanceolate, fleshy, reddish-green leaves with white margins. In summer, this species has a beautiful, profuse florescence, which is orange-red and blooms on terminal clusters. The plant reaches an overall height of about 40 in (100 cm).

Antirrhinum

4–12 in

VI–V

SNAPDRAGON

If you squeeze the flower of Antirrhinum majus carefully between thumb and forefinger, it opens like a small mouth, hence the common name Snapdragon. The plant comes in a wide range of colors and lends cheerful, bright tones to balcony boxes and tubs. Whether you combine your Snapdragons with plain, white-flowered plants or blooms of a similar color, the creative possibilities are endless.

The plant can reach the majestic height of 80 in (200 cm). Here, however, we concentrate on the more compact species suitable for growing in pots and tubs. These grow to about 4–12 in (10–30 cm) and are bushy to cushion-like or hanging. The leaves are elongated and dark green. During the flowering period between June and October the white, red, yellow, pink, orange, and even two-tone flowers appear on erect racemes.

In a sunny position, the Snapdragon will show a real propensity to flower, but will also do well in partial shade. It should be watered regularly, but avoid water logging at all costs. By continually removing spent flowers, you will be able to enjoy the florescence right into the fall.

Argyranthemum frutescens

10 in–3 ft

V–X

Marguerite Daisy

Argyranthemum frutescens, also known as Chrysanthemum frutescens or Marguerite Daisy, is a standard tub plant that enjoys a high degree of continued popularity due to its robust nature.

These evergreen sub-shrubs have bluish-green, deeply divided leaves. Depending on the species and cultivar, the foliage can have either pure green or more silvery-gray tones. From May through October the long-stemmed daisies appear, which can be white, yellow, or pink. With species that have golden yellow flowers, these can actually be of the genus Euryops (closely related to the Argyranthemum family) whose flowers are known as Yellow Marguerites. Removing spent flowers regularly and

over-wintering the plant in favorable conditions (bright and cool) can enable it to bloom all year round.

Marguerites bloom best in a position in full sun. It is important to keep them watered during the flowering period. Profuse bushes or tall-stemmed varieties are very popular and attractive, as they can be planted as focal points in ornamental tubs. They combine very well with smaller plants like speedwell, petunias, and pelargonium. Species with lighter growth are also suitable for balcony boxes.

Aristolochia durior

16–33 ft

VI–VII

Dutchman's Pipe

Aristolochia durior owes its common name to its interesting flowers, which look like little tobacco pipes. The flowers, however, are a rather inconspicuous, yellowish-brown color, and are mostly hidden under the leaves. The ornamental foliage of this climbing plant, on the other hand, is very popular for providing greenery for walls and fences and it also creates an ideal, natural screen.

Depending on the climbing support and size of pot, this vigorous plant can attain a height of 16–33 ft (5–10 m). The deep-green, ornamental leaves are shaped like broad hearts, layered densely on top of each other. The flowers, with which the plant attracts insects, appear between June and July.

Dutchman's Pipe is relatively easy to grow. It does not tolerate very strong sun, thriving instead in a sheltered position in partial to full shade. The large evaporation surface of the leaves means that it needs a lot of water, especially in summer.

No matter where you want to enjoy the lush foliage of Dutchman's Pipe, it is important to ensure you have appro-

priate vertical supports. Tension wires and trellises are
equally suitable for this purpose.

Bambusa ventricosa

6–10 ft

Bamboo

With all the different varieties of the Bambusa family, you can enjoy lush, evergreen plants that were originally native to tropical Asia, Africa, and America. On balconies and patios, Bamboo adds an exotic touch of the Orient. Bamboo flourishes in a sunny to partially shaded position. The soil should always be kept moist, particularly in summer, when the shoots are beginning to burst out. Over-watering to the extent that root balls become soaked is just as damaging as prolonged dryness.

The species Bambusa ventricosa is particularly spectacular and ornamental. This type of Bamboo is characterized by thick, bulging internodes (shoot segments between two joints or nodes of the stem) that have given rise to the common name Buddha Belly. This feature becomes more pronounced under poor conditions, caused for example by an overly small container or too little water and nutrients. The linear-lanceolate, dark-green leaves are also very attractive and grow to approximately 5 in (12 cm). In its natural environment, this Bamboo can often grow to over 33 ft (10 m), but in a tub it stays at a height of 80–120 in (200–300 cm).

Begonia tuberhybrida

6–20 in

V–X

Tuberous Begonia Group

Once only used as indoor plants, Begonias are now great, multi-purpose, flowering plants. Native to South America, they are easy to hybridize, so their cultivation has created a huge selection of cascading and upright varieties, with double or single blooms in every color apart from blue and violet. Planted in tubs and boxes, they can give beautiful accents to patios and balconies; there are also species suitable for hanging baskets.

Tuberous Begonias are famous for their extended bloom time that stretches from May through October. It is always astonishing to see the blaze of colors emerging within a few weeks from the unprepossessing tubers. The flowers, some shaped like roses and some like anemones, are up to 4 in (10 cm) in size and the petals can be quite ruffled and frilled. The asymmetrical, dark-green leaves, divided into two uneven halves by the midrib, sit on thick, fleshy shoots.

As Begonias are not winter-hardy, they are not planted outdoors until mid-May. To bring forward the bloom time, plant the tubers in pots as early as April and keep them indoors until May. Once the threat of frost is over, the plants can be put outside.

Your Begonia will prefer a position in partial shade, making it suitable for balconies and patios with morning or evening sun. In addition, the plant needs quite a lot of water. The soil should always be kept slightly moist and fertilized occasionally. Species with large flowers should be supported with stakes and spent flowers should be removed regularly.

There is a huge range of Tuberous Begonias, subdivided according to their growth habit and flower properties:

- MULTIFLORA GROUP: Tuberous Begonia with small flowers; growth height 6–8 in (15–20 cm); flower size 1–2 in (2–4 cm); takes the sun well

- MULTIFLORA—MAXIMA and FLORIBUNDA GROUP: Tuberous Begonias with medium flowers; growth height 8–12 in (20–30 cm); flower size 2–3 in (5–9 cm)

- GRANDIFLORA-COMPACTA GROUP: Tuberous Begonias with large flowers; growth height 12–20 in (30–50 cm); flower size 4 in (10 cm)

- FLORE-PLENO PENDULA or PEN-DULA GROUP: Hanging or Pendulous Begonias forming slender, hanging shoots; eminently suitable for growing in flower baskets

Beta vulgaris

12–20 in

VII–X

Swiss Chard

If Swiss Chard has been somewhat forgotten as a vegetable, it has at least become a favorite decorative plant in recent years. Its large leaves not only taste great, but are distinctly ornamental—a feast for both the eyes and the taste buds.

With Swiss Chard, there are basically two different types of cultivar—Stem Chard and Leaf Chard. The leaves of both varieties are prepared in the same way as spinach, so that both the petioles and leaf-veins can be used in cooking.

The leaves of the plant are erect, long-stemmed, either wrinkled or smooth, and light to mid green. The attractive stalks in Leaf Chard are mainly yellow and, in varieties of Stem Chard, can be white or vibrant red. Swiss Chard grows to an overall height of 12–20 in (30–50 cm).

On a balcony or patio, Beta vulgaris prefers a sheltered position in the sun or in partial shade. It should be sown in good-sized containers at the end of April. The soil in the pot or box should always be kept nice and moist. Leaf chard can be picked two months after sowing; for stem chard, allow three.

Bidens ferulifolia

6–26 in

V–X

APACHE BEGGARTICKS

Bidens ferulifolia is simply indispensable for balconies. Hardly any other gives such vibrant and lasting splashes of yellow. In combination with red and blue flowering plants especially, it offers charming possibilities for color enhancement. This species is also low maintenance, but in hot weather it does need some attention, as it cannot tolerate dryness.

Native to Mexico and southern Arizona, this member of the Daisy family is one of the most vigorous and profuse balcony plants, as well as the frequent plant of choice for hanging baskets.

The leaves of Apache Beggarticks are pinnate, covered with a soft down, and mid-green in color. Dozens of multiple branching, herbaceous shoots grow out from the center of the plant, atop which are the flowers. The flowers themselves consist of a simple corolla of golden yellow, with acute petals arranged around a slightly darker center. They give out a pleasant, sweetish smell, which attracts lots of bees.

Bidens ferulifolia produces flowers over a very long period. With its trailing shoots, it transforms balcony boxes and hanging baskets into a sunny splash of yellow the whole summer long. A mass of golden flowers appears between May and October. This plant will continue to bloom effortlessly, with new blossoms replacing the faded ones even without your assistance.

Varieties of this species are also known as "Golden Eye" and "Golden Goddess." Their abundant, sunny-yellow florescence goes together well with red or violet petunias, heliotropes, and fan flowers. You can produce pretty combinations with blue bindweed, blue daisies, and white-flowered, hanging geraniums.

Bougainvillea

3–10 ft

V–IX

PAPER FLOWER

This ornamental plant is named for the French navigator, Louis Antoine de Bougainville, who discovered it in South America. It is also known by the common name Paper Flower. With its exuberant mass of brightly colored bracts, Bougainvillea gives a real vacation mood to your balcony or patio.

The plant grows like a shrubby vine. In a tub, it can reach the impressive height of 120 in (300 cm). It has ovate to lanceolate, mid-green leaves. The relatively small, single flowers are white and fairly unprepossessing, but are surrounded by gorgeous bracts in stunning shades of violet, red, white, orange, or pink. The bloom time is from May through September.

For Bougainvillea, you should always pick the warmest possible position in full sun, where the plant will be sheltered from wind and rain. The shoots should also be tied to trellises or stakes for support, giving them something to wind themselves around. During the growing season, you should water this plant liberally, but without saturating the soil.

You can work Bougainvillea to good effect with other brightly colored plants like oleander or even hibiscus, but it also looks good when combined with ornamental foliage plants such as palms.

There are a great many species and varieties of this attractive plant. For tub plants, Bougainvillea glabra is a very good choice. Popular cultivars are the robust, violet-flowering "Sanderana," or the white-flowering "Snow White." Slightly more delicate, but just as ornamental, are the cultivars of the Bougainvillea x buttiana species: "Golden Glow" (yellow bracts, fading to orange), "Mrs. Butt" (dark red), and "Scarlet Queen" (crimson).

Brugmansia

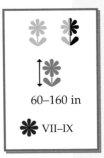

60–160 in

❋ VII–IX

ANGEL'S TRUMPET

With its huge, impressive flowers, Brugmansia (formerly also known by the botanical name Datura) is for many people one of the most attractive and popular patio plants. In the evening, when it exudes its incomparable, intoxicating fragrance, it engenders a relaxed, mood.

Its common name is undoubtedly attributable to the trumpet-shaped, nodding, sometimes pendulous flowers that can grow to 20 in (50 cm) in length. Depending on the species and variety, you can admire the color palette ranging from white through apricot, pink, and golden yellow between July and September. These shrubs or small trees have mainly large, ovate to oblong, dark-green leaves. Angel's Trumpet grows to an overall height of 60–160 in (150–400 cm).

A sunny to partially shaded position sheltered from the wind is ideal for Angel's Trumpet. As it needs a lot of

WARNING——POISONOUS!

Nearly every part of the Angel's Trumpet plant is extremely poisonous! If you have small children, they should not be allowed near these plants unsupervised; alternatively, choose a different patio plant that is not toxic. If the scent of the Angel's Trumpet is breathed in for too long and too deeply, it can lead to dizziness and headaches in those who are more susceptible.

water and nourishment during the growing season, you should water it liberally and frequently as well as regularly giving it fertilizer. Faded and spent flowers and leaves must be removed on a daily basis. For over-wintering, cut the plant right back, then keep it in a dark spot like a cellar or garage.

When arranging it creatively on your balcony or patio, it is a good idea to position the plant to achieve the full effect of the magnificent flowers. The following examples represent the most popular species and varieties.

- BRUGMANSIA AUREA: Also known as Golden Angel's Trumpet, this species is characterized by exceptionally large leaves. Depending on the variety, its flowers can be white, apricot, pink, or golden yellow.

- BRUGMANSIA SUAVEOLENS: This species is also known as Scented Angel's Trumpet. Examples of popular varieties are the yellow-flowering "Golden Dream" and pink-flowering "Pink Dream."

- BRUGMANSIA SANGUINEA: As the name suggests, Red Angel's Trumpet has mostly reddish-yellow to orangey-red flowers.

Buxus sempervirens

BOXWOOD

Also known as Common Box, Buxus sempervirens has played a significant part in garden design and landscape gardening for a very long time. Ornamental and woody, it is not only suitable as a bedding plant for borders, but is also a very popular patio plant. Its branches, densely packed with dark-green, shiny leaves, make it an attractive companion to various ornamental flowering plants all year round.

If you plant Boxwood in flower tubs however, the restricted space for the roots limit its growth to 12–80 in (30–200 cm), which is substantially smaller than its natural height. It has small, ovate leaves that exude a rather strong smell, especially in warm weather. The fairly understated, yellowish flowers appear from March through May. All parts of this plant, particularly the leaves, are poisonous.

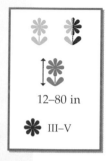

12–80 in

❋ III–V

Boxwood is relatively undemanding and easy to maintain. It is equally comfortable in full sun or partial shade and can even become accustomed to shady spots. During the growing season, it must be watered in moderation, but should not be allowed to become too dry. Throughout the year, pruning will keep the bushes compact.

If you are feeling a little more creative, you can set the stage with these little trees by sculpting them artistically into balls, spirals, pyramids, or cones.

The dwarf cultivar "Suffruticosa," common name English Boxwood, is particularly good for planting in tubs, as it only grows to a maximum height of 40 in (100 cm). Compact in growth, it has medium-size, extremely lustrous, evergreen leaves.

WARNING—POISONOUS!

All parts of the Boxwood, particularly the leaves, are extremely poisonous! If you have small children, they should not be allowed near these plants unsupervised; alternatively, choose a different patio plant that is not toxic.

Camellia japonica

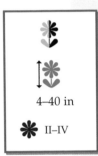

4–40 in

II–IV

Bellflowers

The delicate flowers of this charming plant resemble small bells, giving it its common name and the genus name Campanula, which also means "bell" in Latin.

Campanula has green, heart-shaped to lanceolate leaves, which in some species are covered with thick hair. As well as blue and violet blooms, there are also white and pink

ones; the flowering period is from May until September.

Quite undemanding and relatively easy to maintain, this plant prefers a warm and sunny position, but it can also do well in partial shade. As it does not tolerate a soaking, it should only be watered very sparingly. It is advisable to remove spent flowers regularly.

Depending on the species and variety, Bellflowers can grow to a height of 4–40 in (10–100 cm), though the low-growing plants are more suited to balconies and patios. A short description of two such examples is given below:

- CAMPANULA POSCHARSKYANA: Also known as Serbian Bellflower, this variety is low growing and therefore well suited to planting in tubs. The plant produces prostrate, thick carpets of star-shaped flowers. The trailing shoots can grow up to 24 in (60 cm) in length and provide a distinctly ornamental look when cascading from flower baskets. Popular cultivars are, for example, the white-flowering "E.H. Frost," which grows to about 6 in (15 cm), and the blue-flowering "Blue Waterfall."

- CAMPANULA PORTENSCHLAGIANA: Due to its place of origin, this species is also known as the Dalmatian Bellflower; it grows to a height of about 4–6 in (10–15 cm). A well-known variety is the lavender-blue flowering "Birch Hybrid."

Campanula

4–40 in

V–IX

BELLFLOWERS

The delicate flowers of this charming plant resemble small bells, giving it its common name and the genus name Campanula, which also means "bell" in Latin.

Campanula has green, heart-shaped to lanceolate leaves, which in some species are covered with thick hair. As well as blue and violet blooms, there are also white and pink ones; the flowering period is from May until September.

Quite undemanding and relatively easy to maintain,

this plant prefers a warm and sunny position, but it can also do well in partial shade. As it does not tolerate a soaking, it should only be watered very sparingly. It is advisable to remove spent flowers regularly.

Depending on the species and variety, Bellflowers can grow to a height of 4–40 in (10–100 cm), though the low-growing plants are more suited to balconies and patios. A short description of two such examples is given below:

- CAMPANULA POSCHARSKYANA: Also known as Serbian Bellflower, this variety is low growing and therefore well suited to planting in tubs. The plant produces prostrate, thick carpets of star-shaped flowers. The trailing shoots can grow up to 24 in (60 cm) in length and provide a distinctly ornamental look when cascading from flower baskets. Popular cultivars are, for example, the white-flowering "E.H. Frost," which grows to about 6 in (15 cm), and the blue-flowering "Blue Waterfall."

- CAMPANULA PORTENSCHLAGIANA: Due to its place of origin, this species is also known as the Dalmatian Bellflower; it grows to a height of about 4–6 in (10–15 cm). A well-known variety is the lavender-blue flowering "Birch Hybrid."

Campsis radicans

Trumpet Vine

6–10 in

VII–IX

Originally native to North America, this plant owes its common name to its ornamental flowers, which are shaped like little trumpets. They make this profusely flowering climbing shrub a colorful eye-catcher, creating exotic touches on your balcony or patio.

The Trumpet Vine has bright green, pinnate leaves that guarantee decorative value even outside the flowering season. From July through September, it produces dazzling, orange-red blooms that grow to a size of 2–3 in (6–8 cm) in length.

With its anchoring roots it can usually climb walls and screen without any help, but younger plants benefit from a climbing frame or stakes for attaching the shoots. Planted outdoors, the Trumpet Vine can grow to 33 ft (10 m), and even in a tub it can reach the grand height of 80–120 in (200–300 cm).

Ideally, choose a sunny spot sheltered from the wind for your Trumpet Vine. During the growing season, make sure you water it liberally, and add fertilizer weekly until

August. It is a good idea to remove spent flowers on a regular basis.

Canna indica

1–10 ft

VI–X

INDIAN SHOT

If you want to give a somewhat exotic splash to the flower display on your balcony or patio, you cannot go wrong with Canna indica, also known as Indian Shot. The large, vibrant flowers of this plant, which is native to tropical and sub-tropical America, provide gorgeous touches of color.

Canna indica is a bushy, erect, herbaceous perennial with large, ovate to lanceolate leaves of dark green, sometimes reddish-brown. Between June and October, Indian Shot adorns itself with racemes or panicles of gladiolus-like flowers.

There are many different hybrids of Canna indica whose flowers cover a range of shades from vibrant red through delicate orange to yellow. The flowers can also be single or multicolored. Depending on the variety, the plants grow to 12–80 in (30–200 cm) in height.

Indian Shot prefers a position in full sun, sheltered from the wind, in well-fertilized soil. The soil in the tub should never be allowed to dry out completely, so regular and generous watering is important. By removing spent flowers you can achieve lasting florescence. For over-wintering, cut Canna indica right back and keep the tubers in a dark and frost-free environment.

For planting in containers, it is best to choose a low-growing variety that will only grow to about 20–40 in (50–100 cm). Examples of these dwarf varieties are "Lucifer," with its red flowers edged in soft yellow; "Caballero," whose yellow flowers are speckled with red; the yellow flowering "Salsa;" red flowering "Strasbourg;" and "Sunburst," ranging from pink to salmon shades.

Capsicum

1–5 ft

V–VIII

BELL PEPPER

The genus Capsicum, which belongs to the Solanaceae family, is primarily cultivated as a vegetable. Both the plant and the fruit are referred to as "Bell Pepper," while there are other names for the fruit to mark the differences in spiciness, size, and color. So as well as the various ornamental and spice varieties of Bell Pepper, Capsicum also includes the hotter cayenne and chili. The range of species and varieties available is huge. A general rule is that the smaller the fruit, the hotter it is.

In addition to the use of Capsicum as a vegetable plant, we must not forget its highly ornamental value for balconies and patios. The fruit, which varies in size and shape according to the species and variety and is mostly colored in vibrant shades of orange and red, is very attractive.

These herbaceous annuals or short-lived perennials have alternate, lanceolate to ovate, mid-green leaves. Between May and August, white or yellow bell-shaped flowers appear, which start to produce the pendulous, generally rounded fruits from about the end of July. As a rule, these are initially green, and then turn yellow, orange, or red as they ripen. Capsicum can reach a height of 60 in (150 cm).

As this plant is sensitive to cold, it is best to propagate it in a warm room inside or buy it ready established as a young plant. It can then be set out from May onward. As Capsicum has very deep roots, make sure your container is sizeable in this regard.

Native originally to Central and South America, this plant grows best in a sheltered position in full sun. Especially during the growing season, it should be watered liberally, but it will not tolerate a soaking. Spraying the flowers regularly will promote fruit production.

Cassia didymobotrya

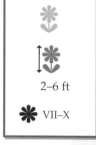

2–6 ft

VII–X

PEANUT BUTTER CASSIA

One of the most noticeable features of this species of Cassia is the erect umbels covered with brilliant yellow flowers, rising out of the foliage like candles.

The long bloom time from July through October can be extended into the next spring with careful over-wintering: for example, in a conservatory. Another specialty of this evergreen shrub is the multiple pinnate leaves that fold in on themselves in the evening to protect against heat loss. If you touch them gently, an intense aroma of peanut butter is produced, giving the plant its common name. Cassia can grow to about 24–80 in (60 –200 cm).

This plant, which is native to Africa, loves a warm position in full sun, sheltered from the wind. Depending on the ambient temperature, the plant should be watered moderately to liberally; the root ball must never be allowed to dry out.

As well as Peanut Butter Cassia, Cassia didymobotrya, another very popular variety is Cassia floribunda. This plant produces cup-shaped rather than candle-shaped flowers, however, and is distinguished above all by its decorative yellow blossoms.

Citrus

CITRUS PLANTS

There is hardly any other plant that embodies the dream of sunny southern climes more than Citrus, in all its varieties. It is no surprise that these beautiful plants are mainly found in warm regions, around the Mediterranean for instance. It is especially effective to combine it with other plants reminiscent of the Mediterranean, such as oleander, bougainvillea, and hibiscus.

All Citrus plants are either shrubs or trees whose twigs—spiny to varying degrees—have slightly leathery, evergreen leaves. White flowers, sometimes tinged pinkish-purple, sprout from the leaf axils: you can admire them between March and September or even all year round in ideal conditions. No less decorative of course are the fruits, usually edible, which then develop from the flowers. In tubs, the plants reach a height of 40–120 in (100–300 cm).

The different species of Citrus should be located in a spot in full sun that is sheltered from both wind and rain. When watering, you have to find a happy medium, as the root ball drying out is to be avoided just as much as water logging. All citrus plants are non-hardy. During the freezing months, they should therefore be kept in a bright, frost-free place like a stairwell. The following examples are a brief introduction to the best-known species.

3–10 ft

III–IX

■ CITRUS AURANTIUM: From the beautifully scented flowers of this species, we get the fruit known as the Seville Orange, or Bitter Orange, because of its sharp taste. It looks like an orange, but is smaller and has a thicker rind. The fruit is inedible when raw, but can be used to make jellies, liqueurs, and candied peel. If you are short of space, the low-growing variety Citrus myrtifolia, known as the Myrtle-Leaf Orange, is recommended.

■ CITRUS LIMON: The species in question here is Lemon, a plant that grows mainly as a small tree. Everyone will be familiar with its bitter fruits, fist-size and yellow or yellowish-green, which develop from the scented flowers.

■ CITRUS RETICULATA: This small, bushy-growing species bears sweet Mandarins, vibrant orange in color.

■ CITRUS SINENSIS: The sweet, round fruit of this species is the famous Orange.

■ CITRUS X PARADISI: This is Grapefruit, valued especially for the juice from its yellow, slightly sour fruit.

Clematis

5–15 ft

IV–IX

Traveler's joy

Clematis has been enjoying greater popularity in recent years. The reason for this lies no doubt in its magnificent, elegant blooms, which have made it the "Queen of Climbing Plants" in the eyes of many admirers. Nowadays, there is an almost bewildering array of species available in stores. The various species and varieties are mainly differentiated by their growth, leaf shape, flowering time, and the shape and color of the flowers.

These ornamental plants can display their true splendor on balconies and patios if planted in the right size of containers. You must also provide them with an appropriate form of support, such as trelliswork, twines, wires, stakes, or chain-link fencing. Depending on the species and ambient conditions, the plant can reach a height of about 60–200 in (150–500 cm), even in a tub.

Originally, Clematis was a plant found in woods, so it makes sense that it likes a position in partial shade. Ideally, this location should also provide the flowers with some light, while at the same time keeping the root area as cool and shady as possible. To ensure this "cool root run," you can cover the plant in the tub with low plants, stones, or a layer of mulch.

Particularly during the growing season, Clematis needs plenty of water and should therefore be watered regularly. As it is sensitive to over-watering, you should make sure the tub has good drainage.

For cultivation in containers, it is a good idea to go for the less profuse wild species or hybrids. Briefly, here are some suggestions for the type you should look for:

- CLEMATIS ALPINA: This early-flowering species, also called Austrian Clematis, produces its violet-blue flowers between April and June, and grows to about 80–120 in (200–300 cm).

- CLEMATIS MACROPETALA: This deciduous species also produces its blue to lavender-blue flowers from April through June, and reaches a height of 80–120 in (200–300 cm).

- CLEMATIS "THE PRESIDENT": This profuse hybrid has very large, blue to purple flowers that bloom from June through September. It grows to 80–120 in (200–300 cm).

- CLEMATIS "JACKMAN III": This late-flowering hybrid produces its purple to violet-blue flowers between July and September, and grows to about 120 in (300cm).

Cortaderia selloana

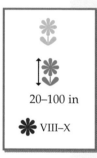

20–100 in

VIII–X

Pampas grass

Cortaderia selloana, also known as Pampas Grass, is one of the most beautiful ornamental grasses for creating a focal point on a balcony or patio. A good container plant, it offers a charming background for—and accompaniment to—brightly colored balcony flowers. But in a solitary position as well, this attractive grass is extremely effective with its conspicuous plumes.

Pampas Grass grows as a dense, upward-thrusting bush. The long, narrow, arching leaves are mid-green in color with sharp margins. The elongated panicles are very ornamental, with small, silky white or pink heads. They appear between August and October, depending on the species. The plant can reach the magnificent height of 20–100 in (50–250 cm).

Examples of extremely attractive varieties are "Pumila" (48 in/120 cm) with its silvery white plumes; "Sunningdale Silver" (up to 100 in/250 cm) with its ornamental, feathery, silvery-white plumes; or "Rosea" (80 in/200 cm) which has lovely, pink plumes.

Cortaderia selloana thrives in a sunny, warm position. It should be watered regularly, but as the plant is sensitive to over-watering, you must ensure good drainage in the container.

Cycas revolute

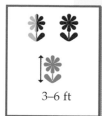

3–6 ft

Japanese Sago Palm

This "dinosaur" among plants belongs to the oldest living group of plants in the world. Related, but now extinct, species of Sago Palm are said to have existed 300 million years ago. Cycas revoluta grows very slowly indeed, making it a modest and undemanding container plant. Whether in combination with other ornamental foliage plants or as a companion to flowering plants, the imposing Sago Palm is always sure to attract attention.

The plant forms a strong shoot with a rosette of attractive, evergreen leaves. These stand erect, but arch gently outward at the tips. It has dark-green, pinnate fronds like ferns. In older specimens, flowers can develop in the center of the leaf rosette. The Sago Palm is dioecious, which means that a plant has either male or female flowers. Male plants develop cone-shaped stamens, while female ones have brown, foliate carpels covered in dense hair.

The ideal spot for the Sago Palm is bright, but sheltered, in partial shade. It can, however, do well in shady positions. The most important requirement is that it is completely protected from wind and rain. The Japanese Sago Palm needs bright and frost-free winter quarters.

Cyclamen

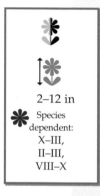

2–12 in

Species
dependent:
X–III,
II–III,
VIII–X

Cyclamen

With its elegant and unusual flower shape, Cyclamen is one of the real pot-plant classics. Some species of Cyclamen owe their popularity not least to the fact that they bloom continuously from October through March, a time when other plants have long since stopped producing flowers.

Many people consider Cyclamen primarily as an indoor plant, but it also feels at home in an appropriate position on a balcony or patio. In winter, it is best to put the plant beside a bright, but cool, north- or east-facing window, as it cannot tolerate the air from central heating or strong sunlight. There are, however, hardy species that can remain outdoors.

Cyclamen thrives in a position in partial shade. For this reason, they are eminently suitable for planting under tall stems or shrubs. While it is flowering, the roots must not be allowed to dry out. Be careful, however, not to water on top of the bulb, as this can cause root rot if the water lies in the

well of the tuber. Spent, faded leaves and flowers must be removed by twisting them off.

- CYCLAMEN COUM: This winter hardy species sometimes flowers as early as February. Its rounded leaves are glossy and unspeckled, or dark green, mottled with silver. The color of the flowers ranges from white through pink to deep crimson red. The plant grows to a height of 2–3 in (5–8 cm).

- CYCLAMEN EUROPAEUM: The so-called European Cyclamen grows to 4–6 in (10–15 cm) and has ornamental, round- to heart-shaped leaves that are often marbled silver above and mainly purple below. The very fragrant, pink to crimson-red flowers of this winter hardy plant appear in August.

- CYCLAMEN NEAPOLITANUM: Also known as Cyclamen hederifolium, this winter hardy species blooms from September until the first frost. The flowers are deep pink, pink, or white. The plant has attractive leaves with pretty patterning, and grows to a height of 4–6 in (10–15 cm).

- CYCLAMEN PERSICUM: This species is characterized by rounded, heart-shaped, dark-green leaves, marbled gray through silver. The flowers, in colors ranging from white, pink, and red through purple, appear in late fall and can bloom throughout the winter, if you bring the plant indoors before the first frost. Cyclamen persicum grows to a height of 8–12 in (20–30 cm).

Dahlia

DAHLIA

Native to Mexico, this plant was named after the Swedish botanist, Andreas Dahl. With its large, ornamental blossoms in a wide range of colors and color combinations, Dahlias are some of the most popular decorative plants. Until late fall, when other plants have long since ceased flowering, lovely Dahlias will ensure a continued splash of color for your balcony or patio.

A huge selection of hybrids is now available in stores. They vary not only in terms of their growth height and leaf form, but also, and primarily, in the size, shape, and color of the flowers. The spectrum ranges from red through pink, orange and yellow to violet and white. Depending on the variety, the plants grow in height to 8–52 in (20–130 cm).

This plant prefers a sunny spot, sheltered from the wind, and should be watered liberally and fed regularly. Spent flowers should be removed. Dahlias are wonderfully suited to growing in tubs or boxes. Keeping them on balconies and patios has the added advantage that you can bring these non-hardy plants into their winter quarters without removing them from their container.

From the array of different pure species and hybrids, you would do best to go for the lower-growing hybrids for containers. Here are a few recommendations:

- MIGNON DAHLIA: Mignon Dahlias grow to a height of 12–16 in (30–40 cm). They are single-headed and bloom profusely.

- TOPMIX DAHLIA: these plants also grow to 12–16 in (30–40 cm). They are single-headed and their growth is compact.

- FIGARO: only reaches about 12 in (30 cm) in height; it is available with double or semi-double flowers.

8–52 in

VII–IX

Diascia-Hybriden

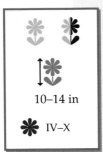

10–14 in

IV–X

TWINSPUR

If you like pretty plants with loosely spaced flowers, then Twinspur is just the right one for you. With its elegant, trailing shoots it makes an excellent choice for balcony boxes and hanging baskets.

The growth of this native to South Africa is compact and bushy, reaching a height of about 12 in (30 cm). Long stems rise up out of a dense rosette of dark-green, glossy leaves. Each stem has several pink or purplish-pink flowers with yellow and green throat spots and two horn-shaped spurs on the underside.

Twinspur is fairly robust. With the correct care, you can enjoy its cheerful flowers throughout the summer.

The plant grows best in a warm position in full sun. Regular watering is important, and both drying out and over-watering should be avoided. Occasionally cutting back withered stems will encourage new flower growth.

The delicate flowers of Twinspur should not be combined with heavier-looking flowers. So suitable neighbors, for example, would be blue daisies or blue bindweed, or others like yellow-flowering tickseed or creeping zinnias.

Dryopteris

2–4 ft

WOODFERN

The Common Fern (Dryopteris filix-mas) is native to the temperate zones of Europe, Asia, and America. The rootstock and petioles of Woodfern, especially young plants, are poisonous. In earlier times, the extract of the plant was used medicinally as a teniacide to treat tapeworms.

Woodfern thrives best in a semi-shaded, sheltered position. As far as care is concerned, it is fairly undemanding, and even tolerates dryness. Its feathery leaves can create beautiful effects on a balcony or patio: for instance, they can be used as an ornamental break between different bright colors in flowering tub plants.

- DRYOPTERIS FILIX-MAS: The Common Fern has mid-green fronds with green midribs. Depending on the variety, the plant can grow to a height of 24–48 in (60–120 cm).

- DRYOPTERIS AFFINIS: The long fronds of the well-known species, also called Golden-Scaled Male Fern, have attractive, golden-brown scales, particularly beside the shoots. The plant grows to about 32–36 in (80–90 cm).

■ DRYOPTERIS ERYTHROSORA: In spring, this species known as Fall Fern produces beautiful, orange-red shoots. Later it turns a glossy green. It can grow to 12–32 in (30–80 cm) high.

■ DRYOPTERIS SIEBOLDII: This species, also known as Siebold's Woodfern, has a peculiar shape for a fern. Its gray-green fronds are only single pinnate.

Eruca sativa

ROCKET, ROQUETTE

Rocket, or Arugula, is a salad vegetable, which has become well known by its Italian name "Rucola" in the last few years as a result of the increasing appetite for Italian cuisine. The tender leaves with their characteristic nutty, peppery taste can be enjoyed on their own with just Parmesan and olive oil, or as an herb in green salads.

This annual plant is shaped like a rosette and has lobed or deeply crenellated leaves. These are elongated and dark green in color. The plant generally grows to a height of 4–8 in (10–20 cm).

You can grow this delicious plant quite easily yourself in balcony boxes and pots. To do this, sow it directly in the appropriate plant container any time between April and September. The seeds should be covered quite lightly with soil. The best position for growing is in full sun or semi-shade. Keep the soil evenly moist, but avoid over-watering. Depending on the heat and weather, you can start to reap the harvest three to five weeks after sowing. It is better to pick the young, tender leaves, as the taste of the older ones can spoil very quickly.

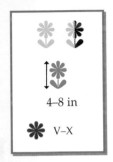

4–8 in

V–X

Erythrina crista-galli

3–10 ft

VII–IX

COCKSPUR CORAL TREE

For those looking for a distinctly ornamental tub plant that is also relatively easy to keep, Erythrina crista-galli is a very good choice. The exotic-looking flowers are particularly striking, characterized by the coral-red color that gives this plant its common name.

The shrub grows to a height of about 40–120 in (100–300 cm) in a tub. Often it has spiny branches with long-stemmed,

mid-green, pinnate leaves, which are each made up of trifoliate, elliptical leaflets. Between July and September, the profuse, long racemes appear, densely covered with red, solitary flowers.

Native to Brazil and Argentina, the Cockspur Coral Tree feels most at home in a position in full sun, sheltered from wind and rain. During the growing season, water it liberally, but take care that it does not become waterlogged.

When designing your balcony or patio garden, placing the Cockspur Coral Tree in a solitary position will create a very special, eye-catching effect. The gorgeous, brilliant red flowers also go well, of course, with other tropical-looking plants such as palms. For over-wintering, cut the trunk right back and store in a frost and light-free place.

Fargesia

3–15 ft

BAMBOO

The evergreen species of Bamboo belonging to the genus Fargesia originate from the humid forests of central China and the northeastern Himalayas.

Depending on the species, Bamboo prefers a sunny to semi-shaded position in rich soil. Care should be taken to

use a fairly large container with an adequate drainage layer, as the plants have to be kept evenly moist, but usually react sensitively to becoming waterlogged.

This ornamental Bamboo is especially effective when given a solitary position to attract the eye. With its interesting foliage, this evergreen plant evokes an air of the Far East. When its feathery leaves rustle gently in the breeze, an extraordinary effect is produced.

- FARGESIA MURIELIAE: An upthrusting plant, this Bamboo has yellowish-green shoots that later turn yellow and branch usually within the first year. When covered in foliage, they have a tendency to bend downward under the weight of the small, bright green leaves. The leaf sheaths are covered in downy hair. The plant grows to about 40–160 in (100–400 cm) in height. Beautiful varieties include "Jumbo" (120 in/300 cm); "Dragon" (also 120 in/300 cm); "Simba," which grows to around 60–100 in (150–250 cm); and "Bimbo," which only reaches a height of 40–60 in (100–150 cm).

- FARGESIA NITIDA: This slow-growing species forms a dense clump of erect, deep-purple canes with powdery culms. It has a loose, pendulous growth habit. Its relatively small, narrow, lanceolate, dark-green leaves give it a particularly graceful appearance. The plant can grow as high as 200 in (500 cm), but in a tub it stays at 80–120 in (200–300 cm). Fargesia nitida should be kept in partial shade.

Ficus carica

3–12 ft

IV–IX

Common Fig

Since ancient times, the sweet fruit of the Fig tree has been prized as a delicious and nutritious food. It has also been used as a symbol of prosperity and fertility. The Fig tree even appears in the Bible as one of the most frequently mentioned plants. Today, Fig trees are still grown all round the Mediterranean and their popularity has spread throughout Europe and beyond.

While Fig trees can develop majestically in the wild, in tubs they remain bushy and grow to a height of about 40–160 in (100–400 cm). The characteristic large, deciduous leaves, which are palmate and have three to five lobes, are especially attractive. On the other hand, the tiny flowers that appear on the tree between April and September are very inconspicuous, as they are hidden in the leaf axis. From these, pear-shaped, purplish or greenish fruits then develop.

The plant needs a sheltered, warm position. Until the new leaves are fully grown, the plant should be kept out of overly strong sunlight, though later it will tolerate full sun. It should be watered liberally and fed regularly during the growing season. The Fig does in fact tolerate some frost, but still benefits from some winter protection.

There are many different ways in which you can use Fig trees on a balcony or patio. If you are creating a more Mediterranean feel, then of course combining it with other plants typical of this region—such as oleander, hibiscus, or citrus plants—is an option. For a tropical touch, you will achieve the desired effect with fuchsia, for instance, or similar plants with brightly colored, exotic flowers that form a lovely contrast with the decorative foliage of the Fig tree.

Fragaria ananassa

8–12 in

✹ VI–VII

Garden Strawberry

In spite of the name, from a botanical point of view the Strawberry is not actually a berry at all, but what is known as an "accessory fruit." The red part of the fruit is actually the thickened floral axis. The real fruits are the yellow achenes embedded in the red flesh.

A wide range of species is now available, which are also good for growing in pots, hanging baskets, and balcony boxes. You can cultivate them in special strawberry pots or troughs as well. These are tall containers with niches all round that can hold several plants at once, thus saving on space.

Strawberries need a sunny position sheltered from the wind. You should use a light soil and water the plant regularly, adding a slow-release fertilizer in spring. The fruit can be prevented from rotting by covering the earth with straw.

The harvest period can be extended by combining different varieties. Some of the popular cultivars of garden strawberry are: "Honeoye"(ripens early); "Annapolis" (large fruit, ripens early); "Tristar" (early variety, medium-size fruit); "Cabot" (big fruit, medium/early); "Lateglow" (late variety with large fruits); and "Allstar" (late variety with small fruit).

Fuchsia

Fuchsia

In Germany, Fuchsia is commonly called "Bell Bush" for its most delightful feature, its flowers—resembling delicate, pendulous bells their magnificent abundance captivates garden lovers throughout the summer. Nowadays, this plant group is so widespread that it is scarcely perceived any longer as an exotic, even though it originated in the mountain regions of tropical Central and South America.

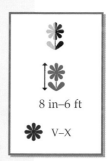

8 in–6 ft

V–X

Fuchsias are all half-hardy annuals, with multiple branching, pendulous shoots and elliptical, dark-green leaves. From May through October, they produce pink, red, purple, or white flowers that can be single, semi-double, or double. The flowers grow as a corona with sepals sitting over it like a frock coat in either the same or a different color. This characteristic structure is undoubtedly the reason for the special charm of these delicate plants, and has inspired growers to develop more and more new varieties. There are now thousands of different cultivars.

These very popular, unproblematic plants are ideally suited to gardens, balconies, and patios. Fuchsias prefer a position in semi-shade in summer and to over-winter at 39–46 °F (4–8 °C). Water them liberally during the growing season, but avoid the root either becoming waterlogged or drying out. Occasional feeding and soaking are recommended. Spent flowers should be nipped off and new growth pruned back.

Fuchsia trees are great favorites now as patio plants. In addition, they are excellent for creating interesting and beautiful visual effects on balconies. The following are some of the huge range of Fuchsia species worth a brief mention:

- FUCHSIA FULGENS: One of the most common species, with bushy growth and reaching a height of 36–72 in (90–180 cm). It has pendulous, scarlet-red, and exceptionally long, tubular flowers.

- FUCHSIA MAGELLANICA: This scarlet Fuchsia is the parent plant to a whole range of hybrids. The species is particularly heat tolerant. Its pendulous flowers are violet-blue and red and have long stamens.

- FUCHSIA TRIPHYLLA: A low-growing, bushy variety, 16–24 in (40–60 cm) in height, with brilliant, coral-red flowers.

- FUCHSIA HYBRIDA: Also known simply as Fuchsia. This designation includes most of the cultivars produced from hybridization. They can be erect or pendulous; bushy or like small trees. The growth height is in the range 12–60 in (30–150 cm) and the color of the flowers spans white, red, and pink to blue and violet. It is suitable as a balcony plant and for all kinds of containers.

Gazania

16–12 in

V–IX

Treasure Flower

The lovely, colorful flowers of Gazania are a bit reminiscent of those of Gerbera. Most of them open out in the warm mid-day sun, but remain closed when it is raining or cloudy. They are commonly known as Treasure Flowers.

Gazania has narrow, glossy, dark-green leaves that are often covered on one or both sides with gray, fuzzy hairs. During the bloom time from May through September, the wonderful blaze of Treasure Flowers appears, with their mainly dark centers on erect stems. The color spectrum ranges from white through yellow to pink and red, and there are frequently bi-colored species as well.

Treasure Flowers should be given a position in full sun. The soil in the plant container should be nutrient-rich and well drained, which can be ensured by making a drainage layer of, for example, pebbles or sand.

It is best to water your Gazania in moderation, making sure that it never becomes waterlogged. If you remove spent flowers regularly, new buds will quickly appear in their place. When choosing its plant neighbors for the balcony box or tub, it is a good idea to pick plants with similar needs, such as members of the Aizoaceae family or cape marigolds.

Hedera helix

ENGLISH IVY

One of the best-known and most popular climbing plants must surely be the Ivy. Hedera helix, also known as Common or English Ivy, is one of the most familiar and pervasive varieties in North America. There is a huge range of different varieties, differentiated mainly by size and growth habit, but also by leaf shape and color.

This vigorous, climbing vine normally has three to five lobed leaves, which are broadly ovate to triangular and a glossy, green shade. In older plants, rather inconspicuous greenish-yellow flowers appear roughly between September and November, which then mature into fruit. Although these are poisonous to humans, they provide a source of food for birds during the winter months. Depending on the species and ambient conditions, Ivy can reach a height of about 60–200 in (150–500 cm) when planted in a container.

Long-lived and resistant to frost, this climbing plant prefers a shady to semi-shaded position, and should be kept well moistened during the growing season. Like most other tub plants, however, ivy is sensitive to becoming water-logged. It is a good idea to trim it into shape occasionally, as well as to cut it back properly every so often.

The versatility of Ivy offers many possibilities when designing your plant effects. It is very good for covering walls and screens with greenery. You can also train the ornamental shoots to grow up railings or supports, or tie them onto tall stakes. Ivy is also particularly attractive as a trailing plant, allowing the shoots simply to drape down from flower boxes or hanging baskets. As ivy tends to be a shade-loving plant, it is very good for embellishing darker corners. The ornamental leaves make a wonderful background for flowering plants. With their long-lasting growth, the following species from the countless numbers of Hedera helix lend themselves particularly to cultivation in boxes and tubs.

5–15 ft

IX-IX

- BUTTERCUP: characterized by five-lobed leaves that are bright green in the shade and turn brilliant yellow in the sun.
- GLACIER: small, three- to five-lobed, grayish-green leaves with silvery-gray or cream-colored markings.
- GOLDCHILD: three- to five-lobed, grayish-green leaves with a broad, golden- yellow margin.
- IVALACE: medium-size, five-lobed, dark-green leaves with bright colored veins and wavy or crinkled margins.

WARNING—POISONOUS!

The fruit of the Ivy is poisonous! If you have small children, they should not be allowed near these plants unsupervised; alternatively, choose a different plant that is not toxic.

Heliotropium arborescens

12–20 in

✳ V-IX

Garden Heliotrope

Heliotropium arborescens is also referred to as "Cherry Pie" because of the sweetly fragrant scent of its flowers, which is at its most intense in the evening.

This bushy shrub has broad, ovate to lanceolate leaves, which are olive to dark green in color. From May through September you can feast your eyes on the umbels of dark-blue to violet flowers. As a rule, Garden Heliotrope reaches a height of 12–20 in (30–50 cm).

This plant prefers a position in full sun to semi-shade, where it should also be sheltered from both wind and rain. In terms of watering, take care to that the root ball neither becomes waterlogged nor dries out completely. To ensure prolonged florescence, spent flowers should be removed regularly.

The lavender-blue flowers of Heliotrope create a really beautiful effect when set alongside white-flowering plants. With a bit of patience, you can also train the plant to grow tall, by stabilizing the main stem on a stake. One of the best-known and most popular varieties is "Marine," with its deep-blue, fragrant, vanilla-scented flowers that grow to about 20 in (50 cm) in height.

Hemerocallis

1–4 ft

V-IX

Daylily

Hemerocallis owes its common name, Daylily, to the fact that its individual flowers only last for one day. However, new buds are constantly forming, with the result that you can enjoy its blossoms on your balcony or patio from May through September.

A bewildering array of varieties of this magnificent flowering plant is now available. Bushy in growth, its leaves are either grassy or lily-shaped. The flowers can be spider-like or starry; triangular, round, or double. The colors range from yellow and apricot to red, brown, and blue.

Depending on the variety, Daylilies can reach a height of about 12–48 in (30–120 cm). These relatively robust plants have a special preference for sunny to semi-shaded positions in rich, well-drained soil. Dead flowers should be removed regularly. Some lovely examples from the unbelievable number of hybrids are: "American Revolution" with dark purplish-brown to deep-red flowers; "Corky" with lemon-yellow flowers; and "Prairie Blue Eyes" with mauve-blue to lavender-blue flowers.

Heuchera sanguinea

Coral Bells

Heuchera, commonly known as Coral Bells, is an ornamental plant in terms of both its leaves and its flowers: it has extremely charming flower panicles that stand above the very attractive foliage, which can be a shimmering green to purple color. There is a huge range of varieties and species that differ in flower shade as well as leaf shape and color.

An example of a very ornamental species is Heuchera sanguinea. This mat or clump-forming herbaceous perennial has rounded or heart-shaped leaves that are flat lobed or dentate. Dark green in color, they are sometimes marbled with silver or pale-green markings.

The large, tubular flowers that appear between May and September in open panicles are mostly red, but in some varieties they can also be pink or white. Coral Bells grow in the shape of a cushion to a height of about 12–16 in (30–40 cm).

They do well in a position in full sun to partial shade. The soil used in the container should be rich and moist, but well drained.

Some of the very attractive cultivars include "Ruby Bells" with vibrant, dark red flower panicles or the white-flowering "White Cloud."

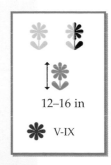

12–16 in

V-IX

Hibiscus

8 in–10 ft

✹ VI-IX

Rose of Sharon

Bunga raya ("great flower" or "festive flower") is the name for Hibiscus in Malaysia, where it is revered as the national flower. In more westerly climes, this ornamental plant with its large, brilliant flowers has become a favorite decorative plant. Especially when combined with other exotic-looking plants, it evokes a warm sensation of the tropics.

Hibiscus syriacus is an eminently suitable species for growing in containers, along with many others, and is also known as Althaea or Shrub-Althaea. This bushy, upright, deciduous shrub has ovate to elongated, three-lobed, coarsely serrated leaves. The axillary, individual flowers appear from August through September and, although they are short-lived, new buds keep springing up to replace them. The color spectrum ranges from red and white to red or purple. In a tub, the plant can reach a height of 80–120 in (200–300 cm).

Hibiscus syriacus should be fed and watered regularly. Rose of Sharon feels most at home in a warm, sunny, and sheltered spot, where it can remain even in winter as long as the tub is well insulated.

A few examples should indicate the huge choice of colors among the different varieties:

- BLUE BIRD: large, violet-blue flowers with a dark red eye

- DIANA: huge, white flowers with a wavy margin

- LADY STANLEY: double, white, pink-tinged flowers with a dark-red center

- RED HEART: white flower with red center

- WOODBRIDGE: large, deep pink flowers with a dark-red eye

Hosta

Funkia

Funkia, also known as Plantain Lily, is appreciated not just for its attractive flowers, which bloom in shades of white, blue, or violet from July to September. The heart-shape to lanceolate leaves are very ornamental as well, and its huge range of hybrids offers a rich palette of shapes and colors.

The long-lived, upright stems can reach a height of 8–36 in (20–90 cm), preferring partial or full shade, so they are made for brightening up darker spots on balconies and patios. Your creative options will also be many and varied with the brightly colored varieties and species of this genus. Here is a brief guide to some of the favorite Hosta species:

8–36 in

VI-IX

- HOSTA CRISPULA: the most notable feature of this species is the huge, heart-shape leaves with white margins that can be as big as 16 in (40 cm). The flowers are lavender blue to lilac in color.

- HOSTA FORTUNEI: with white or violet flowers, the many cultivars of this plant have a range of leaf colors.

- HOSTA LANCIFOLIA: its narrow, lanceolate, dark-green leaves give it its common name, Lanceleaf Hosta. It has violet flowers.

- HOSTA SIEBOLDII: this species has green leaves with a white margin, and is either white or violet flowering.

- HOSTA VENTRICOSA: also called the Blue Plantain Lily, this species has different varieties of green and brightly colored foliage, all of which have violet flowers.

Hydrangea

3–6 ft

VI-VII

Hydrangea

If you want a wonderful sea of flowers on your balcony or patio every year, then look no further than the magnificent and brightly colored Hydrangea. Its distinguishing feature is the huge, ball-shaped flowers, whose shape can vary according to the species—flat-headed, spherical, or race-mose. The plants are correspondingly described as Lacecap, Paniculata, or Mophead Hydrangea.

Hydrangeas do not tolerate strong sunlight well, preferring instead a bright spot in partial shade. Rhododendron soil is just the right type to use in the plant container. During the growing season, the plants should be watered liberally. For this, we recommend you use rainwater or decalcified water, as Hydrangea reacts against high chalk content in tap water by producing yellow leaves. When choosing the tub, you must be sure to provide proper drainage. Spent flowers should be removed regularly.

Hydrangeas are very versatile indeed as part of the design look for your balcony or patio. With their striking flowers, they are best kept as solitary plants, but they are also very pretty when combined with plants with compatible colors such as fuchsia or pelargoniums. Some examples of popular hydrangea varieties that are suitable for balconies or patios are:

■ HYDRANGEA MACROPHYLLA SUBS SERRATA HYBRIDS: the species known as Mophead, or Bigleaf, Hydrangea is a compact, round, deciduous shrub that grows to a height of about 80 in (200 cm). The fleshy, fresh-green leaves are ovate to ovoid-acute and up to 8 in (20 cm) in length. The color of the flowers varies according to cultivar and soil type, from white through pink, red, and violet-red to brilliant blue.

■ HYDRANGEA ASPERA SUBS MACROPHYLLA: this is an evergreen plant, characterized by its large leaves, which are velvety on top and can grow to a length of 14 in (35 cm). The broad, lacecap inflorescence is blue in the center and surrounded by a crown of white flowers.

■ HYDRANGEA PANICULATA GRANDIFLORA: commonly known as Pee Gee Hydrangea, this species also grows to a height of at least 80 in (200 cm) and from

July through August it produces creamy-white, closely packed racemes that gradually age to pink. However, because of its spreading root system, the Paniculata Hydrangea is only recommended for large tubs.

— HYDRANGEA PETIOLARIS: In spite of it name, Climbing Hydrangea can also be grown in a container as a shrub, which can reach a freestanding height of up to 60 in (150 cm). As the name suggests, however, it is really a climbing plant that can ascend a bare wall by several yards using its aerial roots. It takes 5–7 years for the plant to produce its magnificent white umbels, which can grow to 10 in (25 cm) in diameter.

Iberis

4–10 in

IV-V

Candytuft

Iberis is native to southern Europe, where it is found in the wild, usually in rocky places. It makes an impressive container plant, with its distinctive, splendid cushion of white flowers and its highly ornamental, evergreen leaves.

Robust in terms of growth habit, this plant forms dense mats that can grow to 4–10 in (10–25 cm), depending on the species and variety. Its shoots are multiple branched and covered with lanceolate, entire margined, dark-green leaves. Numerous, small flower clusters appear during the flowering period from April to May. The flowers are generally white, but also pink in some species. If you cut back the plant after florescence, it can also bloom again in the fall.

Candytuft is relatively easy to grow. It prefers a position in full sun in loose, rich soil. Good drainage is a must for the plant container. Iberis is an excellent edging plant for balcony boxes and tubs. In larger troughs it soon fills up gaps and provides an ornamental feature.

Well-known species include Iberis saxatilis, also known as Perennial Candytuft or Alpine Candytuft, and Iberis semperviren, or Evergreen Candytuft.

Ilex

2–10 ft

❋ V-VII

HOLLY

The Ilex genus comprises around 400 different species of mainly evergreen, but sometimes also deciduous, trees, shrubs and climbing plants. Holly branches with their attractive, red fruit are a traditional Christmas decoration in Great Britain and North America.

The ornamental value of Ilex lies in the decorative, leathery leaves that, depending on species and variety, can be entire margined, or spiny, uniform green, or variegated in white to cream. Berry-like, mostly black or red, the fruit develops from the unassuming little white to cream-colored flowers that appear between April and June. Though these are very attractive, they are in fact poisonous. If you want to have the pleasure of admiring these beautiful fruit, you should remember that most species and varieties are dioecious, so you will need at least one female and one male plant.

In fall and winter in particular, when many plants have finished flowering or have lost their foliage, the evergreen Holly is a real eye-catcher with its large berries. In their natural habitat, some species can grow into imposing trees 50 ft

(15 m) high. For tub planting, compact and slow-growing specimens are recommended, such as varieties of Ilex crenata or Ilex meserveae, which only reach a height of 20–120 in (50–300 cm).

The attractive Holly thrives best in a position in full sun to partial shade. The soil in the plant container should be moist and very well drained. To keep the soil evenly moist, water the plant regularly. Holly can tolerate a good pruning, so cut it back into shape in the summer.

Impatiens

8–20 in

IV-X

TOUCH-ME-NOT

If you touch the mature seedpods of Touch-me-nots, they immediately burst open, scattering seeds over several feet in all directions. In the wild, this characteristic that gives the plant its name contributes to its rapid propagation. If you are choosing Touch-me-not for planting in flower boxes or tubs, its long-lasting inflorescence of pretty flowers is really the decisive factor, allowing you to admire the splash of colors from May through October.

As well as the many varieties of Bizzy Lizzy (Impatiens walleriana), the New Guinea hybrids—a cross between two varieties native to that country—have now become very popular as well. These upright and bushy growing plants, which can reach heights of 8–20 in (20–50 cm), have very ornamental, flat flowers that can be red, pink, shocking pink, white, orange, or violet, depending on the variety. The light- to dark-green foliage is also very pretty and can have white, yellow, or red markings or venation in some varieties.

Touch-me-not is undemanding in terms of its location, and does equally well in the sun as in partial or full shade. If it is in a very sunny spot, you should be sure to give it enough water. In general, it should be kept at an even level of moisture, as Impatiens does not tolerate wide variations in water provision.

With its wonderful, long-lasting inflorescence, Touch-me-not is suitable for all types of boxes, hanging baskets, and tubs. Naturally, the wide range of varieties allows you to combine all sorts of different colors.

Low-growing varieties are particularly suitable for growing on balconies, such as the orange-flowering "Tango," or "Spectra" with its red, pink, violet, or white flowers.

Ipomoea

Morning Glory

Morning Glory, genus Ipomoea or Convolvulus, is an extremely ornamental climber. It shoots up suitable supports such as trellises, wires, railings, or fences at a rapid rate, reaching a height of 80–120 in (200–300 cm).

The brightly colored flowers that appear between July and October in the dense, fresh-green wall of foliage are extremely pretty. With numerous, mainly heart-shape leaves, Morning Glory is an excellent choice for adding some greenery to seating areas on balconies and patios.

In a sunny spot, sheltered as far as possible from wind and rain, Morning Glory can flourish in its entire splendor. The soil in the plant container must never be allowed to dry out completely, so you should water the plant frequently, especially in the growing season.

A few very ornamental species are:

6–10 ft

VII-X

■ IIPOMOEA LOBATA: Also known as Spanish Flag, or Firecracker Vine, this plant has numerous, small, funnel-shaped flowers with crimson-colored petioles. At first, the flowers are scarlet-red, then orange, before finally turning yellowish-white.

■ IIPOMOEA PURPUREA: Known as Common Morning Glory, this plant has large, mid-green, heart-shaped leaves and trumpet-like flowers up to 2 in (6 cm) in diameter, in red, purplish-blue, or white.

■ IIPOMOEA TRICOLOR: The funnel-shaped flowers of this well-known species of Morning Glory, commonly called Mexican Morning Glory, are blue to purple colored with a creamy-white center.

Lantana camara

1–6 ft

V-X

Lantana

The flowers of this plant, also known as Shrub Verbena, change color during the bloom time. Apart from this unusual feature, they make popular tub plants due to their abundant, long-lasting inflorescence, sturdy character, and the fact that they are so easy to grow.

This fast-growing, evergreen shrub is closely packed with elliptical, dark-green, slightly wrinkled leaves. From May through October, the tubular flowers appear in thick clusters. The varieties range in color spectrum from red, yellow, or white to variegate. The plant reaches a height of about 16–80 in (40–200 cm).

Lantana prefers a sunny to semi-shaded position. During the growing season, it should be fed and watered regularly. To maintain the florescence, spent flowers, as well as the berry-like fruits they produce, should always be removed. Care should be taken when handling the plant, as all parts of it are extremely poisonous.

Grown as a tall plant in a tub, Lantana can be particularly attractive, as this way the magnificent blooms are seen to best advantage. These ornamental plants are also very well suited to planting in hanging baskets or balcony boxes. In addition, their wonderful flowers attract lots of butterflies to a balcony or patio.

Some examples of very popular and well-known varieties are "Athens Rose" (deep-pink flowers with a gleaming, yellow eye); "Confetti" (salmon-colored flowers, also with a yellow eye); yellow-flowering "New Gold;" and "Radiation" (scarlet-red flowers with an orange eye).

Lavandula angustifolia

1–6 ft

❋ VI-VIII

English Lavender

The wonderful scent of Lavender transports you to the south of France, where the plant grows in large fields and the blue carpets of flowers enshroud the whole region in its unmistakable, aromatic perfume. If you want to bring a touch of the Mediterranean to your home, then be sure to get yourself some Lavender.

The antiseptic, soothing, and anti-convulsive properties of Lavandula angustifolia have been appreciated since antiquity, so for a long time it has been grown as a medicinal plant in monasteries or cottage gardens. The fragrant flowers are not only used in the perfume industry, but are also edible— among other things as a constituent of the culinary staple "Herbes de Provence."

Lavender has gray-green leaves that have white hairs underneath and are slightly curled at the margins. From June through August, the violet-blue (but sometimes also white or pink) flowers appear on long, ornamental spikes that can grow to 16 in (40 cm). Lavender can reach a height of about 12–36 in (30–90 cm).

To take full advantage of the wonderful fragrance of Lavender, position the tub or box near to seats where the plant can thrive in full sun. A classic form of ornamentation is a combination of Lavender and roses. Aromatic Mediterranean herbs like thyme or rosemary are also good companions for this plant.

The tall-growing varieties such as "Grappenhall" grow best in fairly large tubs, while the lower cultivars like "Alba," "Dwarf Blue," "Hidcote Blue," or "Rosea" are also suitable for flower boxes or pots.

Ligustrum

Privet

All the species of the Ligustrum genus, commonly known as Privet, are evergreen or deciduous shrubs or small trees. If you put this imposing plant in a solitary position, it displays its beauty to best effect. As it copes well with pruning, Privet is often shaped into pillars or pyramids, or grown as a tall plant. The following are examples of species that are good for growing in tubs:

3–12 ft

VI-IX

■ LIGUSTRUM DELAVAYANUM: This evergreen, compact spreading shrub has ovate-elliptic, dark green leaves. The spheroid to ovoid blue-black fruits develop from the white flowers that appear in June in long panicles up to 2 in (5 cm) long. The plant grows to about 80 in (200 cm).

■ LIGUSTRUM JAPONICUM: this erect, evergreen shrub has dark green, glossy leaves and panicles as long as 6 in (15 cm) bearing white flowers. It reaches a height of 40–120 in (100–300 cm).

■ LIGUSTRUM LUCIDUM: In its natural habitat, the plant known as Glossy Privet can develop into a majestic tree of up to 50 ft (15 m) in height, but grown in a container and depending on ambient conditions, it remains considerably smaller. It has very beautiful, ovate or oval, glossy, dark-green leaves. Its white flowers appear from August to September in panicles about 6 in (15 cm) long, and then develop into ovate-elongated blue-black fruits.

Privet thrives in a position in full sun or partial shade. In summer, especially, the plant needs a lot of water and plenty of nutrients. The soil in the plant container should be well drained.

Lilium

1–6 ft

V-IXI

Lily

Like the rose, the Lily has been especially admired since time immemorial, thanks to its fabulous flowers and wonderful fragrance. As a result, it is valued in many cultures as a symbol of innocence, beauty, and purity. The Lily did not establish itself, however, as a flower culture and cut plant until the 1930s, when large-scale lily growers like Jan de Graaf succeeded in cultivating several thousand hybrids. This made it possible to keep lily varieties that were bred to be less demanding, even in gardens.

As a rule, all Lilies favor a sunny spot, sheltered from the wind. There are, however, some species that are suitable for positions in partial shade. The plants need to be watered regularly, but do not tolerate becoming waterlogged. For this reason, care should be taken to provide good drainage.

When planted in groups in pots and tubs, ornamental Lilies can be a real eye-catcher, and they also attract bees and butterflies. Depending on the species, subspecies or hybrid, lilies can grow to a height of 16–80 in (40–200 cm), though

the shorter types are preferable for planting in pots and boxes. Here are just a few examples:

▬ LILIUM LANCIFOLIUM: Also known as the Tiger lily, this species has lanceolate, scattered leaves on erect stems with purple stripes. The leaves and stem are covered with short, fine, white hairs. From July through August, racemes of nodding flowers bloom in the shape of a Turk's cap, orange-red and flecked with deep purple. The plant reaches an overall height of 24–60 in (60–150 cm).

▬ LILIUM MARTAGON: This species is commonly known as the Turks Cap Lily and grows to a height of 36–72 in (90–180 cm). It has green shoots flushed purplish-red, with whorled, elliptic to inverted, lanceolate leaves. Between June and August, the rather unpleasant smelling, nodding or pendant flowers appear as panicled inflorescences. These are in shades of pink to purple with darker spots or flecks. This species is also suitable for partially shaded spots.

▬ LILIUM REGALE: The Regal Lily, as it is known, reaches a height of 20–72 in (50–180 cm). It has narrow, linear, glossy, dark-green leaves and, from June through July, bears umbels of trumpet-shaped, highly fragrant, white flowers, which are flushed with purple on the outside and yellowish in the center.

- ASIATIC HYBRIDS: These hybrid forms, derived from different Asiatic species, produce flowers in racemes or umbels and are generally unscented. They have alternate, narrow-ovate leaves.

Lobelia

LOBELIA

Named for the Flemish botanist Matthias de L'Obel, the Lobelia is appreciated especially for its brilliantly colored flowers. Depending on the height and shape of the different species and varieties, these ornamental plants are very suitable for balcony boxes, basins or pots. There are also pendant varieties that seem made for hanging baskets. Lobelias also look attractive when planted under taller plants, and also prevent the topsoil from drying out.

Lobelia prefers a position in the sun or semi-shade. The soil in the plant container should always be kept evenly moist, so regular watering is recommended. Two very well-known Lobelia species are:

▬   LOBELIA CARDINALIS: Also known as Cardinal Flower, this species is an herbaceous perennial whose upright growth reaches a height of 24–36 in (60–90 cm). The alternate, lanceolate to elliptic leaves are green and often flushed with a shade of bronze. From July to September, the plant produces its stunning scarlet red flowers.

- LOBELIA ERINUS: This species, known as Edging Lobelia, is grown as an annual and is available in both erect and pendant varieties. The alternate, lanceolate leaves are mid- to dark green. In the bloom time from May through October, a profuse inflorescence of delicate white, pink, violet, or blue flowers appears. The plant grows to about 4–10 in (10–25 cm).

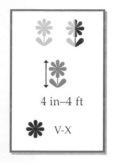

4 in–4 ft

✳ V-X

Malus

3–10 ft

IV-V

CRABAPPLE

Even if you do not have a garden, tasting apples direct from the tree is a treat you must not miss. The less prolifically growing species in particular can be grown in a tub with the proper care. When doing so, be sure to select an appropriate size of container (2–4 gallons/10–20 liters) as even the smaller varieties can grow to 40–120 in (100–300 cm).

The considerable ornamental value of these deciduous trees should not be forgotten. For, depending on the species and variety, Malus comes in the most varied and decorative heights and spreads, such as Columnar, Spindle Bush, Bush, and Dwarf Apple. Another very attractive feature is the white to pink flowers, which often have a beautiful fragrance and appear from April through May. The leaves are oval with an acute tip, deep green, and glossy and most varieties turn wonderful shades in the fall.

As apple trees are generally not self-fertilizing, two or three different varieties must be planted to ensure pollination. With so-called "duo" apples, where two varieties are grafted on one tree, this is unnecessary. The fruits then ripen between August and October.

The plant prefers a sunny position in well-fertilized, well-drained soil. It should be kept evenly moist, so regular watering is recommended, as is cutting back in winter. As the trees normally over-winter outside, look out for frost resistance when choosing your plant container.

If you do not have much space, a Columnar Apple is available, which only grows 12–16 in (30–40 cm) wide, as the short fruit branches sit directly on the trunk. A lovely example is "Flamenco," a fall apple that is red and green, and sweet and juicy.

Melissa officinalis

20–40 in

VI-VIII

LEMON BALM

When you rub the leaves of Melissa officinalis between your fingers, it releases a fragrant scent of lemons, making the origin of its common name very obvious. In times gone by, the herb was also appreciated for its healing properties—for anxiety and insomnia, for example.

This profusely growing herbaceous perennial has ovate, toothed, light-green leaves. It prefers a sunny, warm, and sheltered spot in loamy, sandy soil. While the plant can easily grow to a height of 40 in (100 cm) in the garden, it only reaches about 20 in (50 cm) in balcony boxes or tubs, but quickly overwhelms neighboring plants. The small flowers that bud from July through August on the upper leaf axes are white to pink in color and not especially noteworthy.

The scented leaves of Lemon Balm are best when freshly picked. They have a bittersweet taste of lemon and give a subtle refinement to cold and warm drinks as well as desserts, ice cream, salads, white meat, and fish.

Mentha

1–3 ft

VI–X

MINT

Everyone is familiar with the characteristic, aromatic smell, and taste of Mint, whether from peppermint tea, chewing gum, or lozenges. It is also an important ingredient of the famous English mint sauce.

In summer, especially, Mint is a great addition to the herb garden on a patio or balcony, for the menthol in the leaves has a cooling and invigorating effect. This is why it a popular flavoring for refreshing summer drinks, desserts, soups, and salads.

The properties of Mint that are beneficial to your stomach, as well as its anti-spasm and analgesic effects, also make it a popular medicinal herb. You can pick the leaves fresh throughout the summer.

The plant prefers a moist, humus-rich soil and a position in partial shade to sun. As most varieties spread rapidly through suckers, we recommend you plant Mint in its own balcony box or tub. There it can spread out at leisure without impeding other plants.

A bewildering choice of different species and varieties of mint is now available to us. Two very well-known and popular varieties are briefly described below.

▬ MENTHA X PIPERITA: This variety also goes by the name Peppermint and must be one of the best-known hybrids. This high quality Mint is characterized by its particularly intense peppery scent and flavor. The plant has ovate-oblong leaves with toothed margins and produces its lilac to pink-colored flowers between June and August. Depending on the species and ambient conditions, it can reach a height of 12–40 in (30–100 cm). "Mitcham" is a very popular variety. If you want fruity aromas, choose Orange or Lemon Mint from the group Mentha x piperita citrata.

▬ MENTHA SPICATA: Some of the names by which this species is commonly known are Green Mint, Garden Mint, or Spearmint. Its excellent flavor is explained by the fact that it contains little or no menthol, giving it a subtle aroma and making it more easily digestible. The plant, which grows to 12–40 in (30–100 cm) high, has oval to lanceolate leaves with toothed margins, and produces its pink to pale lilac flowers from July through October. "Spearmint" is a very well-known variety used to flavor chewing gum, mouthwash, and toothpaste.

Narcissus

DAFFODIL

Like other bulbous plants, Daffodils are a cheery addition to springtime, with their beautiful colors and intoxicating fragrance. This enchanting plant was named for the beautiful youth, Narcissus, who was in love with his own reflection and subsequently turned into a flower. A huge selection of Narcissus species and varieties is available nowadays, of which the smaller and more ornamental wild variants are more suited to growing in balcony boxes and tubs.

In general, Daffodils grow to a height of 4–18 in (10–45 cm), depending on the species and variety. The flowers, most of which are yellow (though you can also get white and pink ones) mostly grow as a single bloom on a stalk and appear between March and May.

In the fall, plant the bulbs at a depth of 4–6 in (10–15 cm) in an appropriate container, or else buy young plants in spring. Ornamental Daffodils look beautiful when grouped together. They do best in a sunny to semi-shaded position in well-drained, rich soil. Here are a few examples of ones that are good for growing in tubs:

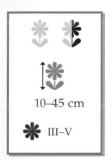

10–45 cm

III–V

- NARCISSUS BULBOCODIUM: This small species of Narcissus only grows to 4–6 in (10–15 cm). It has dark-green leaves and trumpet-shaped, deep-yellow flowers.

- NARCISSUS CYCLAMINEUS: Reaching 4–6 in (10–15 cm) in height, this Daffodil has dark-green leaves and nodding, golden-yellow flowers.

- NARCISSUS TRIANDUS: Also known as Angel's Tears Narcissus, the smaller types of this species that only grow to 4–12 in (10–30 cm) are recommended. The flowers are pale yellow to cream colored, often with several atop each stalk.

Nerium oleander

3–10 ft

❀ VI–IX

Oleander

For that relaxed feeling on your balcony or patio, be sure to
choose Oleander for your container plants, for it is the very
symbol of the sunny south. Its mass of colorful flowers
makes it a special favorite.

This evergreen shrub grows loosely erect to spreading,
and can reach a height of 40–120 in (100–300 cm). Its long,
narrow leaves are dark green. The flowers appear between
June and September as umbellate terminal clusters and,
depending on the species, can be white, red, pink, or yellow.
As all parts of the plant are poisonous, care should be taken,
particularly with small children.

Oleander prefers a position in full sun where it is sheltered from wind and rain. In summer especially it should be
watered liberally. Before bringing it in for over-wintering in
late fall, you can bring it back into shape by removing bare
shoots and trimming those that are too long. So that you do
not lose all the buds that have formed in the fall, it is best not
to trim all of the branches.

If you are thinking of suitable neighbors for Oleander in your garden design, then ideally you should pick other plants that evoke a southern flair. Citrus plants, hibiscus, and bougainvillea are all possible choices, but ornamental leaf plants like palms or box also provide a decorative backdrop for the brilliant splash of color.

There is a huge range of Oleander species with all sorts of shades of flowers. Some examples are the white-flowering "Album Plenum," delicate pink "Louis Pouget," yellow-flowering "Marie Gambetta," salmon-pink "Petite Salmon," and red-flowering "Scarlet Beauty."

Ocimum basilicum

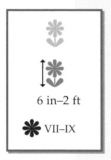

6 in–2 ft

VII–IX

BASIL

The increasing popularity of Italian cuisine is certainly one of the main reasons why no herb garden can now be without Basil. This aromatic herb is the classical accompaniment to tomatoes and mozzarella, but also gives a tasty and visual zing to many other Mediterranean dishes. On a balcony or patio, the leaves provide a touch of the sunny south with their characteristic peppery, spicy fragrance.

Known in some cultures as the King of Herbs, the plant is also said to have medicinal properties: for example, as an appetite stimulant, an aid to digestion, or for the treatment of spasms. Basil grows as an erect, branching plant. The elongated leaves are oval and gently curved. From July through September flowers appear in shades from white to pink. Depending on the species and ambient conditions, Basil can reach a height of 6–24 in (15–60 cm).

Thanks to the growing demand for Basil, there is now a wide range of cultivars available in stores. With European Basil there is a distinction between the small-leaved, very aromatic and larger-leaved, more resistant variety. Red-leaved Basil is particularly captivating, not only giving dish-

es a hot and spicy taste, but also ensuring visual accents of decorative color. Fans of Oriental cuisine will reach for the spicy-aromatic Thai Basil. Other scented variations like Lemon or Aniseed Basil are also available.

The simplest and quickest way of adding Basil to your herb garden is to buy pots in a garden center or supermarket and then repot them at home in balcony boxes or tubs. The plant prefers a sunny, sheltered spot in warm, humus-rich soil. In summer it should be watered regularly. If you want to grow Basil from seed, you should note that it needs light to germinate. Between March and April, spread the

seeds out, ideally on a warm window ledge or in a green-house, and cover them lightly with soil.

It is best to pick the young shoots and leaves before the plant flowers from June onward. It is customary to sprinkle them fresh on dishes just before serving, as they lose color and aroma when heated. Basil can also be dried, though it is not as fragrant. It is better to freeze the chopped leaves, in an ice tray for instance, in order to preserve that summery taste.

Olea europaea

Olive Tree

6–10 ft

VI–VIII

More than just about any other plant, the Olive Tree characterizes the Mediterranean landscape. It is no surprise then that olives, the fruits of this tree, represent the most important economic products of that region. For many travelers, the attractive foliage is a reminder of moments that they would like to relive at home.

This evergreen grows tall very quickly, but then branches out slowly. In a tub, it reaches a height of about 80–120 in (200–300 cm). The most ornamental part of the Olive Tree is its beautiful foliage. The leaves are dark green above and silvery-white and hairy beneath.

On the other hand, the small, creamy-white flowers that appear between July and August are fairly inconspicuous. Olives can only develop if another variety is present to pollinate the plant, as the flowers themselves are infertile. The delicious fruit needs very warm and balmy temperatures in order to ripen.

The plant is relatively easy to grow, preferring a warm spot in full sun that is sheltered from wind and rain. When growing outdoors, the roots of the Olive Tree reach deep into the earth and can still find water through periods of drought. In a tub, however, take care that the tree does not stay dry for too long: water it regularly, but do not allow the root ball to dry out or become waterlogged. The plant tolerates pruning well, so feel free to cut it back or trim it into shape.

Combined with typical Mediterranean plants like oleander or some citrus plants, you can use Olive Trees to good artistic effect. A larger tree in a solitary position will also work as a very attractive focal point.

Origanum vulgare

8–28 in

VI–X

OREGANO

The classic pizza herb! Origanum vulgare, also called Wild Marjoram, should be familiar to most people as Oregano. Like basil, this aromatic herb is one of the most important flavorings in Italian cuisine. Its characteristic taste is not only great for flavoring pizza, however, for it is also very good for seasoning meat, fish and potato dishes, pasta sauces, soups, and stews.

Oregano—related to marjoram, which is frequently used in other European cooking as well—has lots of small, oval leaves with fine hairs. Pretty little pink or white flowers appear between June and October.

The plant is native to southern Europe and Asia, so its favorite spot is a sunny and warm one. As it tends to spread profusely, use a container with a fairly large diameter when planting it. Oregano can reach a height of 8–28 in (20–70 cm).

You can pick the young leaves and shoots of Oregano at any time, but they are particularly aromatic and pungent during the flowering period. The stems are also very good for drying.

Osteospermum hybrids

DAISYBUSH

Osteospermum, commonly known as Daisybush or African Daisy, is a very popular flowering plant thanks to its long bloom time and pretty flowers, which resemble marguerites. Most species of these evergreen sub shrubs, perennials, and annuals originate from South Africa.

8–16 in

V–X

All of the hybrids now available are particularly sturdy and have strong colors, making them favorite balcony and tub plants.

The shrubs, mainly grown as annuals, are bushy to cushion-shaped in growth habit. They have lanceolate, lush, green leaves. The ornamental flowers appear between May and October, displaying a color spectrum from white through yellow, orange, pink, and red to violet. The plant grows to an overall height of about 8–16 in (20–40 cm).

African Daisies thrive in a sunny position protected from rain in light, medium-rich, and porous soil. The plant should be kept just moist, and certainly not soaked. Spent flowers should be trimmed off regularly.

The magnificent splashes of color of Osteospermum hybrids create attractive effects when combined with other beautiful flowering plants such as Gazania or even hardy ice plants.

Parthenocissus

CREEPER

Creepers are a genus of the Grape family (Vitaceae). The name "Parthenocissus" is a combination of the Greek words for "virgin" and "ivy." And, like ivy, this popular climbing plant is frequently used to provide greenery for house walls. On a balcony or patio you can also use it as a lovely form of visual cover as well as providing shade.

Also known as Woodbine, this plant prefers a sunny to partially shaded position. Planted in the open, it can grow to 40–50 ft (12–15 m) in height and 33 ft (10 m) wide. For growing in a tub, choose a big enough container and cut back spreading growth at the beginning of winter, and even in summer if necessary. In the first few years of growth, Creepers require some form of support.

20–50 ft

VII–IX

The glossy, green leaves of Creepers are mostly three- to five-lobed or toothed, depending on the species and variety. In the fall they turn yellow and then brilliant red, providing a wonderful play of color. The whitish-green flowers are small and unremarkable, maturing in the fall into the blue-black racemes that birds love to eat. On the other hand, the fruit of the Woodbine is unfit for human consumption.

Passiflora

3–10 ft

VII–IX

PASSIONFLOWER

This ornamental plant owes its name—Passiflora or Passionflower—to its flowers, which were believed to be symbols of the Passion of Christ. Thus the violet-white corona was said to represent the Crown of Thorns; the yellow, pentagon-like stigmas were the nails of the Cross; and the reddish-brown styles or tendrils were the wounds of Christ. Some species of Passionflower, such as Maracuja, have edible, delicious fruit.

There are about 400 different species within the Passiflora genus, differentiated primarily in terms of the color of their flowers, leaf shape and color, and type of fruit. All of them are magnificent, evergreen climbing plants with leaves up to 5 in (12 cm) long and convoluted tendrils borne from the leaf axes.

The most striking feature, however, is the ornamental, exotic flowers—some of which can be huge—that appear between June and September depending on the species. The outer tepals are often very vibrant in color, and surround the circular, filamentous petals resembling a corona. Passionflowers can reach an overall height of about 40–120 in (100–300 cm).

This plant prefers a warm, sheltered spot in the sun and should be watered liberally during the growing season. It is a good idea to provide a suitable form of climbing support in the form of frames or stakes. A brief description of some examples of the different species is given below:

- PASSIFLORA CAERUELA: Known as the Blue Passionflower because of its wonderful, violet-blue flowers, this plant is a well-known and widespread species. The variety "Constance Elliot" is white flowering.

- PASSIFLORA EDULIS: This species will be very familiar to many people thanks to its delicious fruit— Maracuja or Passion Fruit. Its flowers are white and purple.

- PASSIFLORA INCARNATA: This is an ornamental species whose flowers have a striking, violet-and-white striped corona. Commonly known as Maypop, it is also known as a medicinal plant: for treating nervousness and insomnia, for instance.

- PASSIFLORA VITIFOLIA: This species produces extremely beautiful, showy scarlet flowers.

- PASSIFLORA VIOLACEA: The flowers of this profusely blooming species are violet.

Pelargonium

10–14 in

IV–X

GERANIUM

Nearly everyone knows Pelargonium by its common, but botanically incorrect, name—Geranium. It has become almost the embodiment of the ideal balcony plant.

And even if Pelargonium has acquired rather an unadventurous image of late, this native to South Africa is still going strong and is by far the pot plant with the biggest sales. Its special popularity is above all down to its versatility, its abundance of flowers, and the brilliant colors of its blooms. In addition, it is very easy to maintain.

Pelargonium blooms continuously, producing their most spectacular inflorescence when located in full sun. It also thrives in partial shade. Even cool, rainy summers do not seem to affect it adversely. These enduring herbaceous perennials can usually be over-wintered well at about 41 °F (5° C).

Many gardening enthusiasts will know Pelargonium from the Peltatum and Zonal hybrids in particular—that is, Pendant or Standing Geraniums. By crossing these two species, hundreds of cultivars with different shades of flowers and varied leaves have been produced.

The plants from the group of Peltatum hybrids known as Ivyleaf Geraniums reach a height of 10–14 in (25–35 cm). They are characterized by their long shoots, which can grow to 60 in (150 cm) and cascade down over the plant contain-

er forming a decorative curtain. For this reason, they are particularly suited to hanging baskets. Countless flowers in
a multitude of shades from white, pink, salmon, red, and
lilac to bi-colored variants provide strong dashes of color
among the green of the lobed foliage. Of the bewildering
array of trailing varieties, those of the "Cascade" group have
become well established.

Upright Pelargonium of the Zonal hybrid group also
offer a huge choice of colors, their leaves being very attractive as well. These are usually marked with a distinctive,

darker band, giving them the common name Zonal Geraniums. Well-known and loved varieties are, for example, "Rio," "Mere Casino," "Pink Champagne," and "Caliente."

As well as these two hybrid groups, scented and ornamental-leaved Geraniums such as Regal Geraniums (known more as indoor pot plants) are becoming increasingly popular again. Yet, whichever ones you decide on, the versatile selection of Pelargonium species and varieties opens up numerous possibilities for creating beautiful effects. Their luxurious growth and stunning blossoms will provide a commanding aspect in balcony boxes, planters, and pots.

Pennisetum compressum

20–28 in

VIII–IX

CHINESE FOUNTAIN GRASS

Pennisetum compressum, or Pennisetum alopecuroides, is commonly known as Chinese Fountain Grass or Swampy Foxtail, two appropriate names deriving from its feathery inflorescence. The wonderfully bushy flowers of this native to Asia also make it a real showstopper of a plant.

The tall and wide, densely compact grass has narrow, grayish-green leaves growing as long as 12–24 in (30–60 cm). The tiny, light to reddish-brown flowers appear between July and September on long, fluffy spikes 6–10 in (15–25 cm) in length. This evergreen plant is a real favorite thanks to its ornamental fruits, which grow long into the winter. This ornamental grass grows to an overall height of 20–28 in (50–70 cm).

Pennisetum compressum likes a position in full sun and nutrient-rich, well-drained soil. You can create fabulous effects on a balcony or patio with this magnificent ornamental grass. It is good in a solitary position and as a structural plant between colorful spring, summer, or fall flowering plants. The spikes also make a popular decoration in fresh or dried flower arrangements. An example of a beautiful, very compact cultivar is "Hameln."

Petroselinum crispum

6–10 in

✳ VI–VIII

PARSLEY

Parsley is one of the best-known and best-loved kitchen herbs there is, so for this reason no cottage garden should be without it. With its fresh, piquant taste, this herb is extremely versatile in cooking: it is a popular ingredient in soups, sauces, and cheese, as well as vegetable, potato, and meat dishes. Like so many other herbs, parsley is reputed to have medicinal properties: for example, to stimulate the appetite, aid digestion, and as a diuretic.

It is now available in stores in both Flat Leaf and Curly Leaf varieties: the former has a stronger, more pungent taste, while the aesthetic quality of the latter makes it a favorite as a garnish or decoration.

Parsley thrives best in a sunny to partially shaded spot. It should be watered regularly. The plant grows in

a tall, wide clump and can grow as high as 6–10 in (15–25 cm). The bushy leaves are either pinnate or curly depending on the variety, and can be freshly picked all year round. After producing yellowish-green flowers from June through August of its second year, the plant becomes inedible.

Petunia

6–12 in

V–IX

PETUNIA

Like Pelargonium, Petunia is one of the absolute classics among balcony plants. For years these ornamental plants have enjoyed immense popularity, providing cheerful splashes of color on balconies and patios with their bright flowers. Through intensive crossbreeding, numerous hybrids have now been cultivated in a vast galaxy of colors and forms.

In terms of growth habit, the basic distinction is between upright and cascading Petunias. Lower, bushy-growing varieties are recommended for planters, balcony boxes, and pots, while those with trailing stems are best for ornamental hanging baskets. A lovely play of color can be achieved by combining Petunias with other typical balcony flowers like geraniums or lobelias.

All Petunias have sticky foliage that almost disappears under the profuse inflorescence. Depending on the variety, the attractive, funnel-shaped flowers can be single or full double, with wavy or fringed margins. Appearing between May and October, they bloom in all possible shades of white, yellow, pink, red, purple, blue, and violet. There are also bicolor varieties.

Petunias prefer a sunny location. We recommend that you water the plants regularly and liberally. On hot days in particular they should never be allowed to dry out completely. If spent flowers are removed, new buds will soon form.

Here is a brief overview of the popular Petunia hybrids:

- GRANDIFLORA F1: these species belong to the upright-growing petunias. Distinguished by their very large flowers they are, however, particularly susceptible to rain damage, so it is best to keep the plants in this group in a sheltered spot. They grow to about 8–16 in (20–40 cm) in height.

- MULTIFLORA F1: these Petunias are also upright-growing plants. They are a little more rain resistant and tolerant of poor weather. Their flowers are smaller, but compensate by appearing in greater quantities.

- SURFINA PETUNIAS: This group of cascading Petunias is valued especially for its weather resistance and sturdy growth. The plants grow to 6–12 in (15–30 cm), and its flower-laden shoots can be as long as 60 in (150 cm).

Phaseolus vulgaris

1–12 ft

VII–IX

COMMON BEAN

Originally native to central and South America, this plant is extremely popular in Europe and North America. Beans are relatively easy to grow and therefore eminently suited to planting in tubs. Black, yellow, and purple species are now available that can also have considerable ornamental value.

This heat-loving plant does best in a sunny position, sheltered from the wind if possible. Allowing the Common Bean to dry out completely is just as inadvisable as letting it become waterlogged. There are two different species of Phaseolus vulgaris—Bush or Pole Beans.

▬ PHASEOLUS VULGARIS VAR. NANUS: The Bush Bean has, as the name suggests, a bushy growth habit and reaches a height of about 12–20 in (30–50 cm). It does not need any form of support for this growth. From the end of July, the delicate, tasty, bean pods develop from its white or violet flowers. They can be picked right into October. Regular picking at the right time will encourage new flower formation.

PHASEOLUS VULGARIS VAR. VULGARIS: Runner Beans, as they are known, are climbing plants with the ability to reach a height of about 80–160 in (200–400 cm) with the aid of the right climbing support. They need more heat and nutrients than Bush Beans, but in return they give a better yield and taste better. The harvest time for this species is between August and September.

Warning!

Beans must never be eaten raw, as they contain the toxic protein phasin. This is destroyed by cooking however, so there is nothing to stop you enjoying the taste of these delicious beans.

Phoenix canariensis

3–10 ft

VIII–V

CANARY ISLAND DATE PALM

The majestic Date Palm will guarantee a southern flair for your balcony or patio. It is a real focal point, and not just in a solitary position. You can achieve a fascinating effect by putting it alongside Mediterranean and tropical flowering plants like oleander, bougainvillea, hibiscus, and angel's trumpet. Other ornamental leaf plants also make very attractive companions.

This plant grows tall and wide, and has a sturdy, coarse trunk. In some species, the feathery palm fronds can grow as long as 120 in (300 cm). The Date Palm is dioecious, which means that the plant is either only male or only female. In a tub, the plant very rarely produces flowers. The small, golden-yellow dates that are formed from them would be inedible anyway. Date palms reach an overall height of 40–120 in (100–300 cm).

Phoenix canariensis prefers a warm position in full sun to partial shade, which should also be sheltered from wind and rain. Plant containers should have good drainage and allow plenty of room for the long roots to develop. During the growing period, the plant needs a lot of water, so you should water it regularly. They are just as sensitive to root drying as to becoming waterlogged.

Phormium

3–15 ft

VIII–IX

NEW ZEALAND FLAX

As you can tell from the common name, Phormium is native to New Zealand. On a domestic balcony or patio it can provide a decorative touch: for instance, when combined with other ornamental leaf plants like agaves or palms.

This evergreen herbaceous perennial forms up-thrusting clumps of linear, creased leaves in colors ranging from yellow to dark green. There are different varieties, some of which are particularly appreciated for their magnificent ornamental foliage. From about August to September, small tubular flowers appear on erect panicles. Phormium can grow to an overall impressive height of 40–160 in (100–400 cm).

The plant thrives best in rich, moist, and well-drained soil, and prefers a position in full sun.

A particularly ornamental variety is "Burgundi," also known by its botanical name Pennisetum setaceum "Rubrum." This ornamental grass only grows to 40–80 in (100–200 cm), making it well suited to planting in tubs. Its burgundy-colored culms and dark-red inflorescence make it very attractive indeed.

Phyllitis scolopendrium

12–16 in

Hart's Tongue Fern

Phyllitis scolopendrium, also known as Hart's Tongue Fern or American Fern, is found in many regions of the temperate zone in the northern hemisphere. The special characteristic of this fern is the entire, undivided, tongue-like fronds, which are no doubt responsible for its common name. They differentiate Hart's Tongue Fern from many other European ferns whose fronds are undivided to multiple pinnate.

Ferns provide a decorative touch anywhere on a balcony or patio. The attractive evergreen Hart's Tongue Fern is therefore an ideal way to bring greenery to dark corners, either in semi- or full shade, where many sun-loving flowering plants cannot flourish. The plant's new leaves that are produced in late spring are light green in color, while the

older ones are a stronger green, and firm and leathery in texture.

Depending on the variety, Hart's Tongue Fern can reach a height of about 12–16 in (30–40 cm).

The plant feels really at home in chalky, humus-rich soil. It should be watered regularly during the growing period to keep the root ball moist at all times, but do not let it become waterlogged occur. It is also a good idea to spray Hart's Tongue Fern with soft, warm water.

Pinus

PINE TREE

In summer, the dark-green needles of the Pine Tree provide an interesting background for flowering plants, and in late fall these ornamental plants take center stage themselves. For instance, they fit in very well on balconies and patios with a Mediterranean theme, and they also look great in pots with various rock garden plants.

The Pine Tree is one of the most unassuming woody plants you will find yet, at the same time, it belongs to one of the most beautiful and varied plant families. Its distinctive feature is the needles, which are mostly long and grow in bundles of two, three, or five. Lovers of light, these trees do not tolerate shade, preferring instead a position in full sun. They should be kept evenly moist. You can leave the plants outdoors in winter, but be sure to use frost-resistant containers and protect the root area.

As ever, the smaller species and varieties are recommended for planting in containers.

- PINUS NIGRA: commonly known as the Austrian Pine or European Black Pine, this is a dome-shaped tree with dense, spreading branches and a dark-brown or black bark. A beautiful dwarf variety is "Pierrick Bregeon." It has a flat-topped habit with fresh green, long needles, and grows to a height of about 40 in (100 cm).

1–3 ft

- PINUS MUGO: There are numerous low-growing variants of this well-known species, which is also called Swiss Mountain Pine or Mugo Pine—"Humpy," "Gnom," "Mops," "Mini Mops," and "Pumilio" are just some examples. They are all half-domed to domed, very slow growing, and only reach 12–24 in (30–60 cm) even after years of growth.

- PINUS PUMILA: this fascinating species is also known as Dwarf Siberian Pine or Japanese Stone Pine. "Glauca" is a very popular variety with its broad bushy habit and bluish-green needles. It grows to a height of about 40 in (100 cm).

Plectranthus forsteri

6–12 in

✳ VIII–IX

SPURFLOWER

Plectranthus is commonly known as Spurflower or Swedish Ivy. With a fragrance like incense it should not be confused, however, with Boswellia, the plant that produces true frankincense.

The trailing shoots of this sturdy shrub can be as long as 80 in (200 cm). Between August and September the fairly inconspicuous, white to pale pink flowers appear. The real ornamental value, however, lies in the heart-shape, deep-green leaves, which generally have white margins. The plant grows to a height of 6–12 in (15–30 cm).

In caring for Plectranthus forsteri, it is best to find the right balance. A sunny to partially shaded spot, as well as evenly moist soil in the container at all times, is a good prerequisite for your plant to flourish well. Becoming waterlogged and having too little light rapidly lead to rot and leaf fall, while too much sun can cause brown flecks on leaves.

With its attractive leaves, Spurflower is often used as a structural plant to separate out and balance the competing colors of flowering balcony plants. For instance, it can be a lovely companion for geraniums or chrysanthemums. Its pendant shoots also make it a natural choice for hanging baskets or as ground cover under taller plants in a tub.

A very beautiful and well-known variety is "Marginatus." It is admired above all for its ornamental leaves, which stand out distinctively with their broad, creamy-white margins.

Plumbago

Leadwort

Behind the rather unattractive common name Leadwort hides a plant that is extremely pretty and has become a treasured container plant thanks to its wonderful, mostly light-blue inflorescence. Placed artistically on a balcony or patio, Plumbago can be a real feast for the eyes.

This half-evergreen shrub has initially upright, then trailing shoots of dark-green, elliptic leaves. The umbellate flowers appear from about May onward and keep on developing right into October. Depending on species, the flower color can vary from a pure sky blue to delicate violet or white. The plant can grow to 20–80 in (50–200 cm).

To make the best visual use of Plumbago as a container plant, cultivate it into the shape of a bush, a tall-stemmed plant, a pyramid, or a trellis. If you have a more elevated position for the tub, such as a wall or column, then you can also grow the plant as a sprawling bush, allowing the trailing shoots to cascade down. A particularly flattering combination is achieved with Mediterranean plants like oleander.

Leadwort prefers a warm sunny spot, sheltered from both wind and rain. Be sure to water the plant regularly and liberally. The root ball must not be allowed to dry out, but neither should it become waterlogged. Spent, sticky calyxes must be removed regularly.

Plumbago auriculata, one of the best-known species of Leadwort, is also called Cape Leadwort. Popular varieties of the species are the white-flowering "Alba" and light-blue flowering "Caerulea."

20–80 in

V–X

Polystichum setiferum

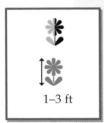

1–3 ft

Soft Shield Fern

Ferns are some of the oldest known plants. They can be found growing wild all over the world and as countless variants. Ornamental ferns are virtually indispensable for brightening up what might be rather unattractive spots out of the sun on balconies and patios. They are both versatile in the ways they can be used and impressive in their shape and texture.

Polystichum setiferum, commonly known as Soft Shield Fern or Alaska Hollyfern, must surely be one of the most elegant species of fern. It forms funnel-shaped, broadly arching clumps, with stems covered in scales and hairs.

Its feathery fronds make this evergreen plant especially attractive. They are multi-pinnate, light green, and soft and matte in texture. This bushy plant grows to an average height of 12–32 in (30–80 cm). Soft Shield Fern prefers a position in partial shade, but will also do well out of the sun if there is enough moisture. It thrives in fresh, humus- and nutrient-rich soil. In summer, especially, it should be watered liberally and sprayed.

Prunus dulcis

SWEET ALMOND

The genus Prunus contains over 200 species of deciduous or evergreen trees and shrubs, including many well-known fruit trees such as plums, cherries, apricots and peaches.

Prunus dulcis, the Sweet Almond, is one of the oldest crop plants. It is primarily grown for its edible fruit, namely almonds, but its flowers are also valued for their ornamental qualities. Anyone who has been on vacation in the Mediterranean region during the almond flowering time is

sure to remember the magnificent sight of the delicate, pink-tinged blossoms.

In a big enough tub situated in a sunny, sheltered spot, Prunus dulcis can thrive, even at our latitudes. Everyone can then bring the Mediterranean spring to their own home.

Sweet Almond is an upright, deciduous tree with lance-olate, dark-green leaves that have finely serrated margins. The beautiful, white to pink-colored flowers appear between March and April on branches that are still bare. Later, they ripen into fuzzy, oval, green fruit with an edible kernel. Outdoors, the plant can grow to a height of 320 in (800 cm), but in a tub it tends to remain about 120 in (300 cm).

If you do not want to miss out on almond flowers in spring, but do not have much space, then you should choose a smaller type, such as "Prunus tenella."

Also known as Dwarf Almond, this cultivar has a bushy, spreading growth habit, reaching only 20–48 in (50–120 cm) in height. This deciduous shrub with multiple stems has finely branched, green-to-brown, shiny, hairless branches.

The leaves with their sharply serrated margins and the wonderful, vivid pinkish-red flowers burst forth between April and May. The ornamental fruits develop from August onward, but in this species they are inedible.

1–10 ft

III–V

Punica granatum

1–10 ft

V–IX

POMEGRANATE

Punica granatum is famous for its delicious red fruit—the Pomegranate. As far back as antiquity, their seeds were celebrated as a symbol of fertility. Today, it is a popular tub plant.

The deciduous shrub or tree has narrow-elliptic, light-green leaves that take on a beautiful reddish shade in the fall. From May through September the striking flowers are formed, mostly red, but also white or orangey-yellow in some species. The fruit can only ripen properly in very warm temperatures. The plant grows to an overall height of about 20–120 in (50–300 cm).

Pomegranate prefers a warm, sheltered spot in full sun. The soil in the tub should be loamy and nutrient-rich. As the plant is very sensitive to becoming waterlogged, choose a container with good drainage. A species well suited to growing in tubs is the Dwarf Pomegranate cultivar known as "Nana," which only grows to a height of 20–60 in (50–150 cm). Its mass of red flowers makes it a very ornamental plant for hanging baskets.

Rhododendron / Azalea

1–3 ft

IV–VI

Alpine rose

The Azalea is a low-growing shrub of the Azalea group, a sub-genus of Rhododendron. While we tend to associate the Rhododendron with 3-ft (1m)-high shrubs in gardens or parks, the Azalea is mainly thought of as a classical indoor plant. There is, however, a whole range of species and cultivars that make excellent balcony and tub plants.

With their glossy, dark-green leaves, these evergreen, broad, bushy shrubs make very attractive ornamental foliage plants. Their true impact, however, comes from their umbellate racemes of brilliantly colored flowers in shades of red, pink, lilac, white, and yellow, providing beautiful accents of color even as early as spring.

Azaleas are not fond of strong sunlight, so you should position them in partial shade. In spring, the plant needs plenty of (preferably soft) water and must be prevented from drying out all year round. In addition, it is advisable to feed it on a monthly basis until late fall, using an acid-based rhododendron fertilizer. Azaleas should be planted in humus-rich, acidic, rhododendron soil. Spent flowers should be removed, but generally cutting back should not be necessary.

Azaleas look particularly beautiful in terracotta tubs. The plant groups suitable for growing in tubs are:

- RHODODENDRON YAKUSHIMANUM hybrids: This species originating in Japan will do well with standard garden soil.

- RHODODENDRON REPENS hybrids: characterized by compact growth, they produce flowers in a stunning red.

Tiny "Diamant" Azaleas are ideal for balcony boxes.

Ricinus communis

CASTOR BEAN

The magnificent palmate leaves of this impressive container plant, light green to dark burgundy depending on the species, are its most stunning feature. The spiny, red capsules, whose

poisonous seeds are used to produce the castor oil are also very ornamental. Combined with other tropical plants, Castor Bean is sure to create an exotic look.

This splendid plant grows as a semi-woody or evergreen herbaceous shrub, or almost like a small tree. As it is so fast growing, reaching a height of up to 120 in (300 cm), the Castor Bean is mainly grown as an annual plant. This makes both cutting back and over-wintering unnecessary. The flowers appear from August through October in tall, terminal, panicled clusters. The yellowy-green male flowers are on the lower part of the panicle, and the reddish-brown female ones in the upper part.

Castor Bean prefers a bright, warm spot, preferably in full sun and sheltered from wind. The soil should be kept moist, as its water and feeding requirements are quite intense, in summer especially.

One very beautiful variety is "Sanguineus." It grows to about 80 in (200 cm) and has green foliage, veined and tinged red, as well as distinctive seedpods of a blood-red color.

5–10 ft

VIII–X

WARNING—POISONOUS!

The seeds of the Castor Bean are poisonous! If you have small children, they should not be allowed near these plants unsupervised.

Rosa

8 in–12 ft

❋ VI–X

Rose

The rose is often called "Queen of Flowers"—rightly so, as it is certainly one of the most elegant and best loved of all decorative plants. For centuries, plant enthusiasts have sung the praises of its fabulous flowers and wonderful fragrance. Unfortunately, not every rose lover has his or her own garden. Much of the bewildering array of different species and varieties now available can, however, also do very well in tubs, boxes, or large hanging baskets on balconies and patios, given the correct care.

Whether you go for a dwarf, bush, full standard, trailing, or climbing variety of Rose, you will be able to take your pick from a massive selection in terms of flower type and color. It is a general rule for all species of Rose that the roots need a lot of space. So you should always choose a large container at least 16 in (40 cm) deep, which is frost resistant if at all possible, for roses can over-winter in a tub given the right insulation.

These plants love a sunny, airy position. They are just as intolerant of high winds and drafts as they are of strong midday sun and a build up of heat. To avoid them becoming

waterlogged when watering, good drainage must be provided. You should also be careful not to pour water onto the leaves. Spent flowers should be removed.

A few examples of the huge range of species and varieties are described below:

- ROSA "BLAZE SUPERIOR": this Climbing Rose grows as high as 120–160 in (300–400 cm), and has gorgeous, crimson-red flowers. It is good for brightening up patio screens or walls, for instance.

- ROSA "GRAHAM THOMAS": At a height of 48–60 in (120–150 cm), this fast-growing Bush Rose makes a beautiful tub plant. The fully double flowers are yellow.

- ROSA "HERITAGE": This species has fully double, antique, delicate pink flowers that have a wonderful fragrance. It grows as a bush, reaching a height of 40–60 in (100–150 cm).

- ROSA "LOUISE ODIER": This bushy Dwarf Rose reaches 60 in (150 cm) in height. The pink flowers are rosette-shaped and have a lovely scent.

- ROSA "ROSMARIN 89": A compact-growing Dwarf Rose only 8 in (20 cm) tall, it has dense, double pink flowers.

ROSA "ICEBERG": This bush rose with radiant, white, double flowers grows to a height of 40–60 in (100–150 cm).

Rosmarinus officinalis

Rosemary

Native to the Mediterranean, Rosemary is an important ingredient in the cookery of that region. This fresh, slightly bitter herb is used to flavor meat, fish, grills, vegetables, and potato dishes.

6 in–6 ft

III–VII

This ornamental plant is a treat for the eyes as well as the taste buds. It exudes its unmistakable scent in summer on a balcony or patio, reminiscent of pine trees.

An evergreen woody shrub, it has narrow, needle-like leaves that are bluish-green in color. From March through July, the pale blue to lilac flowers appear in the leaf axes.

Rosemary thrives best in a very sunny and sheltered spot in humus-rich, loamy, and sandy soil. As the plants tend to dry out very quickly in flowerpots or tubs, you should water them regularly. With the proper care, they can be very long-lived and reach an impressive height of 80 in (200 cm), depending on ambient conditions. Unfortunately this heat-loving herb is non-hardy at more northerly latitudes, so it may have to over-winter indoors.

The leaves and sprigs of Rosemary can be picked as required throughout the year. They are also good preserved in dried form.

Rubus

BLACKBERRY

Above all, the Blackberry is a favorite garden plant on account of its fruit. Its very high vitamin content makes it an extremely healthy fruit that can be picked from high summer until early fall. The fruit is deliciously juicy, can be eaten raw, or else can be made into jam, jellies, compote, or syrup.

Garden Blackberry grows as a woody, spreading shrub. On a balcony or patio it looks good when cultivated against a fence or wall, where it should be supported by a wire frame. The thorn-free (easier for picking) varieties that tend to be lower growing are more suited to tubs.

A sunny to semi-shaded position is ideal. The soil should be porous, so it is advisable to have a drainage layer in the container. When the fruit is forming, feeding and liberal watering are required on a weekly basis. Blackberry is the only berry shrub that should be cut back in June in order to produce fruit in the strong side shoots.

A selection of popular blackberry cultivars are: "Shawnee" (thorny, high fruit quality); "Thornfree" (thornless, slightly acidic, sharp taste); "Loch Ness" or "Nessy" (thornless, good flavor); "Navaho" (thornless, sweetly fragrant).

1–6 ft

VII–X

Salvia officinalis

12–20 in

VI–VIII

SAGE

Salvia officinalis, also known as Garden Sage, is one of the oldest medicinal and culinary herbs. As far back as antiquity, Sage was used as a remedy; this explains its botanical name, which derives from "salvare"—meaning to heal, or to save. The plant is also very ornamental when it flowers and, in good weather, its wonderful, spicy aroma provides a touch of Mediterranean flair.

This semi-evergreen shrub has green to silvery-gray leaves that are generally downy and produces elongated-oval shape, blue-violet flowers from June through August. Its height is in the range 12–20 in (30–50 cm). One very attractive variety of Salvia officinalis is "Tricolor," whose white-margined leaves are flushed with red.

Native to the Mediterranean region, this plant loves a very sunny spot, sheltered from the wind, in loose, rather dry soil. Sage fits in well in the herb section of your balcony or patio, of course, but is also very attractive when combined with flowers of all colors.

Sage leaves can be picked at any time, but they are particularly aromatic in May before the plant flowers. As it has a strong flavor, Sage should be used judiciously as a seasoning. It makes an excellent addition to many Mediterranean dishes and is indispensable in the case of the popular Italian specialty "Saltimbocca" (veal escalope with ham and sage).

There are various other species and varieties of Sage, some of the ornamental ones not quite as suitable as a seasoning, but all the nicer to look at nonetheless. Among others, the brilliant red-flowering Scarlet Sage (Salvia splendens) or the violet-blue flowering Mealycup Sage (Salvia farinacea), whose petioles look as if they have been dusted with flour, are both very attractive.

Sanvitalia procumbens

2–12 in

✳ V–X

CREEPING ZINNIA

The enchanting little flowers of Sanvitalia procumbens, commonly known as Creeping Zinnia, are like tiny sunflowers. The sturdy, abundantly flowering plant is a much loved summer flower, which does equally well in balcony boxes, planters or hanging baskets.

The Creeping Zinnia is a bushy, mat-forming, trailing plant that spreads rapidly. It has fresh green, thick foliage of oval-lanceolate leaves, from which the pretty, golden-yellow flowers with black centers radiate from May through October. The plant grows to a height of about 2–12 in (5–30 cm).

Creeping Zinnia feels at home in a nice, sunny spot. A fairly modest plant that is easy to maintain, it should only be fed and watered in moderation. If you remove spent

flowers regularly, you will be able to enjoy its magnificent blossoms right into the fall.

The cheery flowers are at their most ornamental when the shoots cascade profusely over boxes, hanging baskets, or planters. For this effect, place the plant right at the edge of the container. It is also wonderful as a low-growing plant beneath tall-stemmed ones.

Satureja hortensis

SUMMER SAVORY

In Germany, this herb is commonly known as Bean Herb, which gives an indication of its particular affinity with bean dishes. This is not just because of its strong, peppery taste, but also because it is reputed to be good for the stomach and digestion, making it easier to cope with legumes that are often difficult to digest. Aromatic Summer Savory can be used in many other ways in cooking: for example, as a sea-

soning in potato dishes, stews, pickled cucumbers, meat, and sausages.

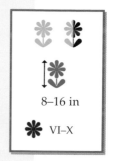

8–16 in

VI–X

A well-known and widespread species of this plant is Satureja hortensis, also known as Summer Savory. With an upright, bushy growth habit, the plant can grow to 8–16 in (20–40 cm). The pungent leaves are narrow, dark green, and have a soft, downy covering. From June through October the small, white or pale lilac-to-pink flowers appear. The whole plant in Summer Savory gives off an intense aroma.

If you find a location in as much sun or partial shade as possible on your patio or balcony, Summer Savory should thrive well in these ideal conditions. The soil should be humus-rich, well drained, and kept regularly watered, though in moderation.

You can start to pick the young shoots in early spring. The aroma of the plant is at its most intense just before and during the flowering period. If you want to preserve a rich harvest of Summer Savory, it lends itself well to drying. For this, you should pick sprigs and tie them together in bundles, then after hanging them up to dry you can pluck off leaves as required.

Winter Savory (Satureja montana) has a slightly stronger, sharper flavor and can be grown all year round.

Scaevola aemula

8–12 in

IV–X

Blue Fanflower

Scaevola derives its common name from its ornamental flowers, which spread out in a semicircle like little fans. The plant is not only easy to maintain and weather resistant, but is also a delight with its non-stop propensity to produce magnificent flowers. These features make it a popular plant for growing in boxes and tubs.

A bushy and sprawling plant, often grown as an annual, it produces shoots up to 40 in (100 cm) long with gray-green foliage. You can enjoy the mass of blue-to-lavender colored flowers from April through October. Scaevola reaches an overall height of about 8–12 in (20–30 cm).

A position in full sun or partial shade is ideal

for Blue Fanflower. It should be watered regularly with rain-water, or soft water, as it does not tolerate any chalk content. It is also sensitive to becoming waterlogged, so be sure to provide good drainage in the container. As its leaves are slightly succulent, short dry periods will not do it any harm.

Blue Fanflower is a fabulous plant for hanging baskets and can easily spread to a diameter of 40 in (100 cm), given the right conditions. In a balcony box, it does not crowd out its neighbors and is therefore eminently suitable for mixed boxes. To create a striking effect with the lavender-colored flowers, try com-bining it with pink or red geraniums, for exam-ple, or yellow-flowering plants like creeping zin-nia or pocketbook plants. A more subtle option to accompany it, though no less attractive, is white daisies or simple orna-mental foliage plants.

Schlumbergera

16–24 in

I–XII

Christmas Cactus

Although Schlumbergera bears only a passing resemblance to cacti in the traditional sense, it does belong to the Cactus family or, more precisely, to the genus of Christmas Cacti. As what is known as a Segmented Cactus, its most striking feature is the flat, serrated leaves that look as if they are chained together. At the end of the last segment of these spineless stems, long flowers of about 2–3 in (5–8 cm) develop, with two symmetrical flower heads. Depending on the species and variety, Christmas Cactus has white, pink, salmon, red, or even violet flowers.

Native to the Brazilian forests, the plant belongs to the epiphytic category of plants, meaning that it is attached to or grows on trees or other plants, without being classed as a parasite.

Christmas Cactus is good for planting on a balcony or patio using humus-rich soil, which should be very porous and preferably sandy. A warm, but not necessarily sunny spot is ideal. Christmas cactus also prefers high humidity through spraying rather than too much watering.

On the whole a very undemanding plant in terms of care, it produces plenty of lovely flowers from November through February, especially if it has already been brought indoors to a cool position at the end of August. It will be happy there without much watering until the first buds appear, when it can be given more water, with an ideal night temperature of about 68 °F (20° C).

Sedum telephium

12–20 in

IX–X

WITCH'S MONEYBAGS

The genus Sedum, known in the vernacular as Stonecrop, contains a bewildering array of species and varieties. One very ornamental species is Sedum telephium, also commonly known as Witch's Moneybags or Orpine. The plant is very popular due to its late bloom time from September to October. So in the fall, when many of the colorful summer flowers have already faded, it provides lovely accents of color.

This herbaceous perennial has upright, bushy growth that reaches a height of 12–20 in (30–50 cm). The leaves are ovate, fleshy, and light- to grayish-green in color. The little pink to purple-colored flowers are grouped together in large terminal clusters.

Relatively easy to maintain, Witch's Moneybags should be kept fairly moist in a sunny position. As this member of the Crassulaceae family can store water in its fleshy shoots and leaves, it does not need daily watering. In spring you should cut back the faded shoots.

Smaller varieties are suitable for balcony boxes, while larger ones look great in ornamental tubs. You can create wonderful combinations with other fall flowering plants or simple ornamental foliage plants.

Sempervivum

2–6 in

VI–VIII

Houseleek

Like nearly all the members of the Crassulaceae family, the evergreen Houseleek is a succulent plant—that is to say, it can store water in its leaves. The name "Sempervivum" comes from Latin; it means "always living," a reference to the long-lived nature of this herbaceous perennial, as well as its hardiness and modest needs, even in difficult growing conditions.

For aficionados of this plant, the decorative value of its many different species—and their countless varieties—lies in their spherical rosettes of fleshy leaves in the most diverse shapes and colors. With their foliage acting as water storage, the plants can survive even long periods of drought without damage.

The flower-bearing stem grows out of the rosette, covered in leaves that are layered like roof tiles. The flowers, shaped like a blazing star, are cymose inflorescences in shades of red, yellow, and—less frequently—white. After flowering, the rosette dies off, but only after producing several offsets: the result is that the plant covers smaller areas with rosettes of differing sizes. Depending on the species and variety, Houseleek reaches a height of 2–6 in (5–15 cm).

These undemanding plants require sandy, well-drained soil and a sunny position. They are particularly ornamental in shallow planters or small troughs, which can also be decorated with a few stones. Combined with other succulent plants like witch's moneybags, you can conjure up a magical little rock garden for yourself on your patio or balcony.

Solanum

1–6 ft

V–X

NIGHTSHADE

The species-rich genus of Nightshade plants, mostly bushy or climbing in growth habit, contains among others the famous food crops, Potato (Solanum tuberosum) and Aubergine (Solanum melongena). It also produces extremely beautiful ornamental plants, which are ideal for growing in containers. A few examples are described below in brief.

■ SOLANUM JASMINOIDES: this species, also known as White Potato Vine or Jasmine Nightshade, belongs to what must surely be the most stunning specimens of climbing plants. This fast-growing, evergreen shrub can grow to a height of 80–200 in (200–500 cm), depending on ambient conditions. Its shoots are covered with broad, lanceolate leaves. Its magnificent inflorescence of white to pale purple flowers is particularly lovely.

■ SOLANUM MURICATUM: this creeping species with lanceolate leaves is also known as Melon Pear or Pepino. The striking fruit that appears in late summer

is just as visually attractive as the mauve-colored flowers. About the size of a tennis ball, it is round and orangey-red to golden yellow in color, and flushed or striped in violet. This juice-laden fruit tastes a bit like melons or pears. All other parts of the plant are poisonous. It grows to a height of 20–40 in (50–100 cm).

- SOLANUM RANTONNETII: this plant has now become one of our most popular species of evergreen shrubs. This is not just because of its inflorescence, which is so profuse that it almost covers the broad, oval leaves. The ornamental flowers are deep mauve with a small yellow eye. This species can grow as high as 120 in (300 cm).

- SOLANUM WENDLANDII: this plant also goes by the name of Costa Rica Nightshade or Giant Potato Creeper. It can climb many feet high using its hook-like spines. Both the large, oval leaves, which can be either pinnate or undivided, and the umbellate, lilac or white flowers are extremely ornamental.

Nightshade thrives best in a sunny to semi-shaded position, sheltered from the wind. During the growing season, you should water the plant liberally and feed it regularly. It is important to note that most of the Solanum species are poisonous in whole or in part. Depending on the growth habit, the plant can be grown as a shrub or on a trellis sunk into the container. Its thick foliage will guarantee an exotic flair for your balcony or patio. Lovely plants to put alongside it are angel's trumpet, lantana, or palms.

Solanum lycopersicum

TOMATO

After the potato, the Tomato (also called Love Apple) must be the most significant food plant of the Nightshade family. Originally a plant growing in the wild, it is native to the South American Andes. The first cultivars are said to have been produced in Mexico: its name derives from the Aztec *Xitomatl*.

Today, there is a huge range of varieties, which differ mainly in terms of shape, size, and weight, as well as of course in taste. It is divided into four main types in relation to its outer shape: Round, Beefsteak, Plum, Pear, and Cherry Tomato. A further distinction is between tall-growing Vine Tomatoes and low-growing Bush Tomatoes.

This annual fruit-vegetable is very easy to grow, and is particularly suited to pot planting on a patio or balcony. It can be sown indoors from mid-March onward and then, once the last frost is over, the plants can be placed outdoors. From May, little yellow flowers appear, from which firstly green fruits develop within a period of about two months,

10 in–4 ft

VII–X

later turning yellow, orange, or red in color depending on the variety.

Tomatoes prefer a position in full sun, sheltered from the wind, if possible in front of a heat-giving wall. The soil should be nutrient-rich and the plant container should hold at least 2 gallons (10 liters) with a diameter of about 12 in (30 cm). During fruit production, you must water the plants liberally and feed them on a weekly basis.

In the case of vining tomatoes, remove (or "sucker") the side shoots to ensure a rich harvest. They will also require supporting stakes or trelliswork. Bush tomatoes on the other hand do not have to be grown tall or clipped, but if the fruit crop is heavy a short stake can increase stability.

Examples of some of the varieties that are especially suited to growing in containers are given below:

- TALL-GROWING, "INDETERMINATE" VINE TOMATOES: "Large Red," "Cherry Grande VF," "Sweet 100" (Cherry), "Marmande" (Beefsteak), "Yellow Pearshaped" (Yellow Pear), "Roma VF" (Yellow Plum).

- LOW-GROWING, "DETERMINATE" BUSH TOMATOES: "Patio," "Balkonstar," "Tumbler" (Cherry Tomato); the last two varieties are exceptionally good for planting in hanging baskets.

Strelitzia reginae

3–16 ft

II–VIII

BIRD OF PARADISE

If you would like to add an exotic touch to your balcony or patio with a flamboyant plant, then Strelitzia reginae is an excellent choice. It is fairly easy to maintain and its long-lasting flowers in magnificent colors provide lots of pleasure. The plant was named botanically for the English queen, Charlotte, the wife of King George III, as she was born the Princess of Mecklenburg-Strelitz. The common name, Bird of Paradise, derives from the shape of the flower, which looks like an exotic bird.

This herbaceous perennial, which grows to a height of 40–80 in (100–200 cm), has long-stemmed, evergreen, elongated-oval leaves. Between February and August the spectacular flowers appear, which can grow to 6 in (15 cm) in length. The inflorescence consists of a sharply pointed spathe, out of which individual orange and blue flowers emerge in the shape of a bird's crest. Indigenous to South Africa, the plant prefers a warm position in the sun, sheltered from the wind. During the growing season, it should be watered regularly, but not to the extent that it becomes waterlogged. A non-hardy plant, Bird of Paradise should be over-wintered in a bright position at about 50–55 °F (10–13° C), and watered only moderately.

Sutera diffusus

Ornamental Bacopa

Sutera diffusus, also known as the Snowflake Flower, is appreciated both for its easy maintenance and sturdy nature as well as its profuse growth with long lasting, abundant inflorescence.

The plant has simple, opposite, small leaves. In the flowering period between April and October, small, star-shaped flowers appear that can be white, pink, purplish-red, or blue depending on the variety. The plant reaches an overall height of about 6–10 in (15–25 cm), while its shoots can be as long as 40 in (100 cm).

Ornamental Bacopa will flower most profusely in a position in full sun, but it will also do well in semi-shade. The soil in the container should be rich and well drained, and should never be allowed to dry out.

With its creeping or trailing growth, it is very effective in both balcony boxes and hanging baskets, which it can easily fill up with its wonderful mass of flowers. In larger containers it can, however, be combined with other standard balcony plants to beautiful effect. The very versatile Ornamental Bacopa is also suitable for growing under taller plants.

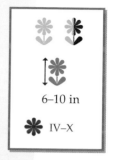

6–10 in

IV–X

Thunbergia alata

Black-eyed Susan Vine

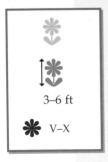

3–6 ft

V–X

Funnel-shaped flowers, golden yellow to orange in color, blaze out from the dark green foliage of this pretty shrub. Their black centers are no doubt the reason for the common name Black-eyed Susan.

Thunbergia alata is mainly grown as an annual ornamental climbing plant with toothed, heart-shape, deep-green leaves. Its magnificent inflorescence blooms repeatedly between May and October. The plant grows to a height of

40–80 in (100–200 cm).

The Black-eyed Susan Vine feels most at home in a warm, sunny spot, which should be sheltered from the wind as much as possible. The plant likes to be watered frequently, but hates becoming waterlogged.

Thunbergia alata can be used in many different ways on your balcony or patio. It is well suited to trelliswork, espaliers, and fences. For these you should provide a form of climbing support—as rough as possible—at an early stage. Alternatively, you can simply plant it in balcony boxes or a similar type of container. Without climbing support, its shoots will trail down, making it a very attractive plant for hanging arrangements.

Thymus

2–12 in

VI–X

THYME

Related to marjoram, Thyme is well known as a delicious herb used in Mediterranean cuisine and is an indispensable ingredient in, for example, many pasta dishes. It is also used as a cure for colds. This aromatic plant is also, however, a good visual addition to flower boxes or tubs on balconies and patios.

These pungent, evergreen shrubs, herbaceous perennials, and sub-shrubs have a bushy growth habit in the height range 2–12 in (5–30 cm). Thyme has narrow-elliptical, grayish-green leaves that are slightly rolled at the margins. The pink to violet-colored flowers can be admired between June and October.

The warmest place in the sun you can find will suit this native to the sunny south; it also prefers sandy, humus-rich, garden earth high in chalk content. During the growing season, it should only be watered occasionally, as Thyme tolerates drought quite well. Its strong aroma protects neighboring plants from pests.

When picking Thyme, it is best not to cut the twigs off too deeply, in order to encourage new shoots. Thyme goes very well with soups and sauces as well as vegetable, meat, and fish dishes, and it is an important ingredient in the seasoning mix "Herbes de Provence." As the relatively small leaves of the plant have low moisture content, Thyme can successfully be dried to preserve it.

There are various species of Thyme that have a wider range of culinary uses. The best-known species is, of course, Thymus vulgaris, usually referred to as Garden Thyme or Common Thyme. Other species are growing in popularity, however, such as Lemon Thyme (Thymus citriodorus) with its characteristic scent of lemons.

Tibouchina urvilleana

3–6 ft

VII–X

Princess Flower

The most striking feature of this native to Brazil, Tibouchina urvilleana (also known as Princess Flower, Glory Bush, or Lasiandra), is without doubt its exceptionally beautiful, deep-purple flowers.

Tibouchina urvilleana stands erect, with few branches and very long shoots. Its large, ovate, deep- green leaves, whose upper sides are covered in velvety down, are also very attractive. The bloom time runs from July through October, but this can be extended by over-wintering in favorable conditions. The flowers are held on terminal panicles or solitary at the end of the shoots. Their shape is very similar to that of large violets. In the wild, the plant can grow as high as 240 in (600 cm), but in a tub it will stay at about 40–80 in (100–200 cm).

Princess Flower prefers sunny locations, but will also do well in partial shade. During the growing season the plant needs regular watering, but be careful to avoid it becoming waterlogged. This also means you should think about appropriate drainage when choosing a container.

To encourage the shrubs to branch nicely and become bushier, you would do well to cut them back and nip off the buds in younger plants. If you plant several specimens together in a larger container, Princess Flower will give the impression of being far bushier.

With its lovely shape and pretty color, the fabulous Princess Flower is sure to grab attention no matter where you put it. Interesting combinations can be created by putting it alongside other tropical-looking plants, such as fuchsia, cassia, angel's trumpet, or nightshade. Even simple ornamental foliage plants like palms make flattering accompaniments to the exceptional blue-violet of its flowers.

Tulipa

4–28 in

III–V

Tulip

The Tulip must be one of the best-known and most popular spring flowers you will find. Since the so-called "Tulipomania," when Tulip bulbs became speculative commodities in Holland in the 17th century, these ornamental flowers have been the very symbol of that country. Indeed, a large part of the demand for Tulips is met by Dutch growers.

Tulips are upright in growth and reach a height of 4–28 in (10–70 cm). They have broad, linear, bluish-green leaves near the ground. During the growing season from March to May, you can admire flowers in colors ranging from white, red, yellow, orange, and pink to even variegated ones.

Originally native to the temperate zones of Asia, this plant thrives in a sunny spot. Some varieties, however, will tolerate semi-shade.

As early as the fall, put the Tulip bulbs into

boxes or planters at a depth of about 4 in (10 cm). If you decide on Tulips spontaneously in the spring, you will find a good selection of pre-forced plants. Tulips should be watered in moderation only, as they will not tolerate becoming waterlogged.

Nowadays, you will often find yourself spoiled for choice when faced with the huge selection of different varieties, species, and cultivars on offer. When buying Tulips, it is best to look at the type of growth and color on the plant descriptor. If you want suitable specimens for planting in boxes or planters, then stick to low-growing Tulips, some examples of which are:

- TULIPA TARDA: This dwarf species of Tulip grows to 4–6 in (10–15 cm) and has star-shaped, creamy-white flowers with a yellow center. The leaves are narrow and mid-green.

- TULIPA-GREIGII HYBRIDS: These hybrids are always the result of crossing Wild Tulips. They have leaves that are either dark with flecks or striped, and grow to about 6–12 in (15–30 cm) in height. In early to mid-spring, the large, cup-shape flowers appear, mostly red or yellow in color.

- TULIPA-FOSTERIANA HYBRIDS: These plants grow to about 6–16 in (15–40 cm) in height and have small, cup-shape flowers. They are mostly brilliant red to orange, with a black fleck edged in yellow.

- TULIPA-KAUFMANNIANA HYBRIDS: This particular plant is sturdy and long lasting, and reaches a height of 6–10 in (15–25 cm). The flowers are often multicolored, with yellow, red, or white predominating.

Vaccinium myrtillus

8–20 in

VI–IX

Bilberry

Wild Bilberry (Vaccinium myrtillus) is also known as Whortleberry or Huckleberry, and is the most common species of Blueberry in Europe. It is characterized by the fruit, which is blue throughout, unlike the American cultivated form—the Blueberry (V. corymbosum)—in which the color is only present in the skin of the fruit and the flesh is clear. The cultivated Blueberry is also bigger than the native Bilberry, but far less fragrant than the wild fruit.

Like their close relatives, cultivated Blueberries and Cranberries (V. macrocarpon), Bilberries can be grown well in a trough or tub. While cultivated Blueberries grow into majestic bushes, the other two species are creeping half-shrubs about 8–20 in (20–50 cm) in height. A popular variety of V. myrtillus is "Top Hat," a mini-bush that can easily be cultivated in a standard pot.

Bilberry plants prefer acidic soil conditions, so rhododendron soil is well suited. This should be kept evenly moist and fertilized regularly. Then, from mid-June through September, the dark-blue, juicy fruit ripens, which is very versatile in cooking—for cakes, compotes, cold fruit soups, and wine, to give just a few examples.

Verbena

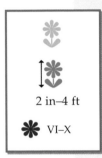

2 in–4 ft

VI–X

Vervain

Folk legend has it that Vervain was used to staunch Jesus' wounds after his removal from the Cross, giving the plant one of its common names, Herb of the Cross. Today, it is a popular decorative plant, mainly because of its long bloom time.

To fully develop its splendid inflorescence, Vervain needs a warm, sunny spot in well-drained soil. It should be watered regularly, but does not tolerate becoming water-logged. Deadheading spent flowers will ensure long lasting florescence.

When choosing from the huge assortment of species, varieties, and hybrids, you should take account of flower shape and color as well as growth habit and height, for these are the decisive factors in terms of its intended purpose. Low-growing hybrids are particularly good for balcony box-es or planters, for example, while species with tall, bushy growth make lovely displays for larger tubs or troughs.

■ VERBENA BONARIENSIS: also called Purpletop Vervain, the especially striking feature of this plant is the small, densely packed, lilac-colored flower clusters. It grows to 32–56 in (80–140 cm) and is therefore well suited to large pots or tubs. In spite of its height, the plant does not take up a great amount of space, as it has no foliage; this gives it a translucent and airy appearance.

■ VERBENA CANADENSIS: this plant has purple or white flowers formed in dense, umbellate inflorescences. It has fresh green, deeply lobed foliage. At a height of 8–16 in (20–40 cm), it is good for planting in balcony boxes or planters; other typical balcony plants such as begonias, petunias or geraniums make wonderful companions for this plant.

■ VERBENA RIGIDA: this particular species is a very good all-weather plant. It has unevenly crenate leaves and lavender to violet-colored flowers on terminal clusters. Its height of 8–14 in (20–35 cm) makes it another suitable plant for boxes and planters. The ornamental blooms go well with those of lavender and sage.

■ VERBENA TENERA: this species has been the parent plant for a whole range of hybrids, which come under the category Hanging Verbena. They have creeping growth with loosely cascading shoots. The height reached by these hybrids, which are ideally suited to growing in hanging baskets, is in the range 2–10 in (5–25 cm).

Viola

8–16 in

III–VII,
X–XI

Violet

Violet is one of our best-known and best-loved flowers. Poets have often sung its praises, and its popularity is second only to that of the rose. There are around 500 species in the Violaceae family. Viola sororia, or Common Blue Violet, grows wild in woods and meadows and is the state flower of Illinois and Wisconsin, among others.

The most distinctive feature of all these species is the characteristic flower, made up of five segments that sit atop

a long stem. The predominant colors are violet, white, and yellow, and the middle, lower petal often has darker markings. The Violets we know as garden plants have developed as a result of numerous hybridizations.

Two species of the large Violet family that enjoy great popularity as plants for pots, tubs, and boxes are:

- **VIOLA CORNUTA:** petite Horned Violet, which blooms relentlessly in an exhaustive range of colors. Following a long bloom time from May to July, the Horned Violet can even flower again in the fall if it is cut back after florescence: this also makes the flower growth more compact. It will thrive in a sunny to semi-shaded position in standard soil mix for balcony plants and can also tolerate periods of drought. Horned Violets are good ground cover for long-stemmed bushes or other tall-growing tub plants, as well as being a colorful addition to brighten up boxes.

- **VIOLA WITTROCKIANA:** Garden Pansies are a treat for the eyes as early as March with their magnificent flowers. The plant prefers a sunny spot and nutrient-rich, loose soil. You should water them regularly but avoid them becoming waterlogged at all costs. Garden Pansies are often combined with tulips, daffodils, hyacinths, and other spring flowers. They are also lovely in larger groups in planters or boxes.

Vitis vinifera

Wine Grape

The Wine Grape is used to produce wine. One of the oldest cultivated crops, it was grown by the Egyptians, Babylonians, and Indians as long ago as 3,500 B.C.E. Even the ancient Greeks and Romans were involved in winegrowing.

This deciduous climbing plant sheds its leaves in winter. In the fall, the three- to five-lobed leaves turn a brownish-red color. The Grapes that appear in September/October are either yellow, light green, or blue-black, depending on the variety.

Wine Grape is very good for planting on patios and balconies. You will, however, need to think of the fair amount of space it takes up. If you do not make a conscious effort to keep its growth down by cutting it back in January/February, this twining plant will grow robustly and rapidly to a height of 280 in (700 cm) and over.

Vitis vinifera needs a warm and sunny position, if possible sheltered on the south side of the house and preferably in deep, humus-rich soil. In the growing season, it must be watered liberally, and thereafter only sparingly. To encourage strong growth, it should be cut back in winter and the new shoots tied to a trellis. Wine Grape can be grown as a single vine or fanned on an espalier.

Gardening Tip

If your priority is to produce delicious fruit, bunches of Grapes that are too tightly packed together should be thinned out with scissors. In order to give the Grapes more sun (increasing their sweetness) and make them ripen more quickly, leaves at the base of the fruit should be removed just before harvest time.

6–30 ft

VI–VII

Washingtonia filifera

5–10 ft

California Fan Palm, Desert Fan Palm

Washingtonia filifera is a standard visual feature on American roads, where you will find these ornamental palms—in the southern states in particular—on many streets and avenues. In Germany, it is known as Priest's Palm, because the lower leaves that have died off cover the trunk right down to the ground, like a priest's vestments. The dried-up foliage is removed, however, in the case of ornamental palms.

The plant has an expansive, spreading growth with a thick, pillared trunk. It has large, rounded fronds divided up like fans, with light threads hanging down from them. The edges of the petioles are sharp-toothed. In a tub you should not expect to see the white or bright pink flowers, unfortunately.

Although Washingtonia can grow over 65 ft (20 m) tall in its natural habitat with the right climate, in a tub it will remain at about 60–120 in (150–300 cm) in height. This palm will thrive best in a sunny position. It should be kept moist in summer, but must not become too wet. For over-wintering, it needs a frost-free position that is not too dark.

Yucca

Yucca

Yucca palms have been firm favorites for many years. Strictly speaking, they are not true palms, as they are actually of the Agave genus in botanical terms. The family comprises about 40 species that are native to the drier regions of North and Central America.

These are all stemmed or stemless shrubs, trees, and herbaceous perennials with rosette-formed foliage. The leaves are usually tough and leathery, often with toothed margins or with thread-like filaments. In more mature plants, erect stems can develop from the center of the rosette, with numerous cup-shape, white- or cream-colored flowers. When grown in a tub however, it is rare to see a Yucca flowering.

Wonderful, desert-like arrangements can be designed on a balcony or patios with these undemanding ornamental foliage plants when combined with agaves, oleander, or pomegranate, for instance. Colorful, flowering tub plants like hibiscus or bougainvillea would also be appropriate.

2–6 ft

VII–VIII

Their strange-looking leaves also make larger specimens suitable for solitary positioning. Yucca thrives best in full sun. The plants should be watered liberally at regular intervals, but not daily. They can survive short-term drought, but not becoming water-logged. Until August, add fertilizer every four weeks and remove withered leaves continuously.

Older Yucca often become very top-heavy so, when repotting, choose a container that is sufficiently stable. Care is advised when handling the plant, as you can easily hurt yourself on the leaf tips, which are very sharp indeed.

Well-known and well-loved species include Yucca aloifolia, Yucca filamentosa, Yucca gloriosa, and Yucca elephantipes.

Index of Latin names

Index of Common Names

Image credits

All photos: Medien Kommunikation, Unna
Photographers: Hermann Hackstein, Raphael Pehle, Jürgen Schossig, Walter Trefzer

Assistants: Yara Hackstein, Carola Struck, Beate Engelmann, Christina Muermann, Mathias Hinkerode, Dietrich Löbbecke

Special thanks to: Regina Albrecht-Imöhl